Demos is E
We produc ... ıkers
and host t ... ıt
20 years ... ın
overarching missi... ople.

Demos is now exploring some of the most persistent frictions within modern politics, especially in those areas where there is a significant gap between the intuitions of the ordinary voter and political leaders. Can a liberal politics also be a popular politics? How can policy address widespread anxieties over social issues such as welfare, diversity and family life? How can a dynamic and open economy also produce good jobs, empower consumers and connect companies to the communities in which they operate?

Our worldview is reflected in the methods we employ: we recognise that the public often have insights that the experts do not. We pride ourselves in working together with the people who are the focus of our research. Alongside quantitative research, Demos pioneers new forms of deliberative work, from citizens' juries and ethnography to social media analysis.

Demos is an independent, educational charity. In keeping with our mission, all our work is available to download for free under an open access licence and all our funders are listed in our yearly accounts.

Find out more at **www.demos.co.uk**.

First published in 2013

Magdalen House, 136 Tooley Street
London, SE1 2TU, UK

ISBN 978-1-909037-37-3
Copy edited by the editors
Series design by Modern Activity
Typeset by Modern Activity

Set in Gotham Rounded
and Baskerville 10

TWENTY YEARS OF IDEAS

Edited by
Ralph Scott
David Goodhart

DEMOS

Contents

Acknowledgements 5
Contributors 7

Preface 11
David Goodhart

1 Demos – many successes but one big failure 17
Geoff Mulgan

2 From multiple intelligences to The Good Project 25
Howard Gardner

3 Sharper vision, in retrospect 31
Ian Hargreaves

4 Vote early, vote often 37
Andrew Adonis and Adam Tyndall

5 Auditing: the explosion goes on 47
Michael Power

6 Reflections on the post-modern state 53
Robert Cooper

7 Why post-liberalism is a dead end in British politics 61
John Gray

8 Britain™ revisited 67
Mark Leonard

9 The social entrepreneur 75
Charles Leadbeater

10 The debate over animals 83
Roger Scruton

Contents

11 Relational justice 89
Danny Kruger

12 The good life 95
Amitai Etzioni

13 Valuing culture 103
John Holden

14 A brief history of personalisation 113
Claudia Wood

15 A house of experiment 119
James Wilsdon

16 Character (revisited) 127
Richard Reeves

17 Building the service nation 133
Sonia Sodha

18 Do something different 141
Mariana Mazzucato

19 The map and the territory 151
Helen Burrows

20 Listening in 157
Jamie Bartlett

21 Demos timeline 163

Acknowledgements

First and foremost, many thanks to our contributors for this collection, who provide an illuminating and entertaining history of Demos within these pages and in so doing, also provide some insights into the politics of the past twenty years.

Thanks to Demos staff and contributors past and present, for providing us with such a rich back catalogue to plunder in compiling this collection. We could have filled a volume this size many times over, which only serves to demonstrate the strength and depth of our previous output. Thanks are also due to our trustees, our associates and all of our funders over the years.

In particular, at Demos we would like to thank Jamie Bartlett and Claudia Wood for their contributions, Duncan O'Leary for his irreplaceable institutional memory and Max Wind-Cowie and Jonathan Birdwell for their regular input and support. Thanks to Matt and Alex at ModernActivity for their patience in designing and producing the collection. And thanks too to Sophie Duder and Rob Macpherson for all their work in ensuring the twentieth birthday went with a bang.

Ralph Scott
David Goodhart
July 2013

Contributors

Lord Adonis
Andrew Adonis is a Labour peer and former Secretary of State for Transport and Minister for Schools. He is the author of the recently published 5 Days In May: The Coalition and beyond *and* Education, Education, Education, *and* Back to Greece: the scope for direct democracy, *published by Demos in 1994.*

and Adam Tyndall
Researcher for Lord Adonis.

Jamie Bartlett
Director of the Centre for the Analysis of Social Media (CASM) at Demos. Author of The Edge of Violence *and* The New Face of Digital Populism.

Helen Burrows
Director of Private Office and a former adviser to Culture Minister Ed Vaizey MP. Author of Risky Business, *published by Demos in 2011.*

Sir Robert Cooper
Sir Robert Francis Cooper, KCMG, MVO is a British diplomat and advisor currently serving as a Counsellor in the European External Action Service, and author of The Post-modern State and the World Order, *published by Demos in 1996.*

Amitai Etzioni
Founder and Director of the Institute for Communitarian Policy Studies at the George Washington University and author of The Third Way to a Good Society, *published by Demos in 2000.*

Howard Gardner
Hobbs Professor of Cognition and Education at the Harvard Graduate School of Education and contributor to Opening Minds, *a Demos Quarterly published in 1993.*

John Gray
Political philosopher and author, whose works include False Dawn: the delusions of global capitalism, Black Mass: apocalyptic religion and the death of utopia, *and* After Social Democracy, *published by Demos in 1996.*

Ian Hargreaves
Professor of Digital Economy at Cardiff University and author of Digital Opportunity, *a review of intellectual property and growth conducted for the Coalition Government in 2010/11. Author of* Sharper Vision, *published by Demos in 1993.*

John Holden
Visiting Professor at City University. Previously Head of Culture at Demos, for whom he wrote Capturing Cultural Value *and* Democratic Culture.

Danny Kruger
Chief Executive of Only Connect, a crime prevention charity, and author of Access Denied? Preventing information exclusion *for Demos in 1998.*

Charles Leadbeater
Demos Associate and a leading authority on innovation and creativity, he is the author of a number of Demos pamphlets including The Rise of the Social Entrepreneur *and* Personalisation through Participation.

Mark Leonard
Co-Founder and Director of the European Council on Foreign Relations and author of Britain™, *published in 1997.*

Mariana Mazzucato
Economist and RM Phillips Chair in Science and Technology Policy at the University of Sussex (SPRU). She is the author of The Entrepreneurial State, *published by Demos in 2011.*

Geoff Mulgan
Chief Executive of Nesta and the founding Director of Demos.

Michael Power
Professor of Accounting and Director of the Centre for the Analysis of Risk and Regulation (CARR) at the LSE, and author of The Audit Explosion *published by Demos in 1994.*

Richard Reeves
Non-resident senior fellow at the Brookings Institute in Washington, DC and a former Director of Demos and Director of Strategy for the Deputy Prime Minister. He is co-author of Building Character, *published by Demos in 2009.*

Roger Scruton
Writer and philosopher, and the author of Animal Rights and Wrongs *published by Demos in 1998.*

Sonia Sodha
Head of Strategy and Policy at the Social Research Unit at Dartington. She was Head of the Capabilities Programme at Demos and author of Service Nation, *published in 2009.*

James Wilsdon
Professor of Science and Democracy at the University of Sussex. James worked at Demos from 2001 to 2008, first as head of strategy, then as head of science of innovation. He is on Twitter @jameswilsdon.

Claudia Wood
Deputy Director of Demos and author of a series of reports on personalisation, including Tailor Made *in 2011.*

Preface

David Goodhart

Anniversaries are useful moments in the flow of time to take stock and find patterns of meaning in the life of an individual or an organisation. There can be a bias towards self-congratulation – 'I/we must have made a difference for the better!' I will try not to over-claim in the following preface.

Political life in Britain would have played out much as it did if Geoff Mulgan and Martin Jacques had never had the idea of establishing a cross-party think-tank of the centre-left in 1993. And, as Mulgan points out inside, its founding idea must be adjudged a complete failure. Nevertheless, these 20 short essays bear witness to the fact that Demos has still left a significant mark.

And like any good, generalist think-tank its imprint has been at two levels: at the level of granular policy and at the level of more grandiose ideas, including the language of politics (although the phrase with which Demos is perhaps most associated, Cool Britannia, was never actually used in Mark Leonard's famous pamphlet, as he discusses in his contribution).

Policy and ideas can often overlap: Demos played as big a role as anyone in providing New Labour with a vocabulary for public service reform as well as specific policy ideas (see Claudia Wood on personalisation). Demos was also there, reinforcing its cross-party credentials, when the Conservative leadership needed some progressive conservative ideas in the run up to to the 2010 election.

Reading the Demos founding document with its ambitious intention to 'change the terms of political debate' one phrase jumps out: 'It is difficult to remember a time when people had so little faith in the political process.' By comparison with today 1993 was a golden age of faith in politics and

Demos' mission to revitalise democracy has turned out to be a liberal baby boomer fantasy. Instead of creating a mass participation democracy full of earnestly deliberating citizens, the less ambitious political priority today is simply to ensure that enough people vote to preserve democratic legitimacy, as Andrew Adonis admits inside.

Perhaps Demos made the common mistake of thinking everyone should be like us; we being the inhabitants of a post-university political finishing school, passed through by hundreds of (mainly) young men and women since 1993, who regard politics as a form of self-expression. It is also possible that Demos was simply ahead of its time and that the ubiquitous spread of sophisticated, interactive technologies will soon start to open up novel forms of democratic participation.

In any case, our commitment to the real demos lives on in our research methods, where we continue to place a distinctive emphasis on consulting the public and sampling public opinion (as Jamie Bartlett describes in his essay). And while the political process may not have evolved as we hoped in the past 20 years, the flourishing of organisations such as Demos has contributed to a more open political eco-system. As political parties themselves have become more cliquey some of the role of connecting to the world beyond Westminster has been sub-contracted to think-tanks.

And we have been a career stepping stone for many both within politics and outside, indeed several of the authors in this collection including Mark Leonard, James Wilsdon and Mike Power mention how their Demos pamphlets transformed their careers. Yet despite its resolutely modern and classless self-image Demos may have contributed less to the democratisation of the political elite than it would like: its main founder was educated at Westminster and Oxford, its current director went to Eton and it has been directed by women for less than 3 out of its 20 years.

I am a Demos new boy, having been at the helm for only around 18 months, but for the sake of simplicity its 20 years can be divided into three periods: the first stage of quirky social democracy (1993–8), the second phase of policy application under Tom Bentley as 'New Labour's favourite think-tank' (1998–2006), then as New Labour waned so did Demos: reducing in size but repositioning itself to speak to the two other main parties in British politics.

And what about today's fourth period? For two decades Demos has been at the heart of the intellectual and party political convergence on a mix of social and economic liberalism. As the journalist Steve Richards said recently, liberalism is the most elastic concept in the political lexicon, but it may be that the next 20 years will require a greater emphasis on what liberalism takes for granted. Instead of the stress on the removal of constraints on markets or individuals, we will need a new focus on 'social glue' to guide us through a period of slow growth, further revolutions in technology, immigration and its human consequences, ageing, and so on.

As left and right have (despite the noise of everyday politics) grown closer, so the gap between politics and the ordinary voter has continued to grow wider. Worrying about how to close that gap was part of the original Demos mission and it remains central to our mission today, even if we now know that inviting people to join citizens' juries is not the answer.

There is in this collection a flavour of the 'beyond left and right' sentiment of the founding document. It is there for example in Richards Reeves's interest in character and Charlie Leadbeater's contribution on social entrepreneurs. I want to build on that and help Demos to develop the ideas loosely associated with the slogan post-liberalism (rather hastily dismissed at birth by John Gray inside).

This is not about returning to a mythological 1950s but rather about helping to foster strong communities and a confident patriotism, reconnecting people to politics in a more grounded way through what they care about most: family, place, work and wages (and debt). Such a post-liberal politics is not hostile to aspiration but prefers to stress the value and dignity of all work: vocation as much as meritocracy, which is working out rather too much as Michael Young predicted.

If there is a thread that runs through the different phases of Demos it is a refusal to underestimate people and an insistence that they should have a say in the decisions that affect them; technocratic adjustments to state and market are necessary but not sufficient. Our current post-liberal emphasis is consistent with this Demos tradition: instead of dismissing people's concerns with welfare or immigration as irrational, we should regard these sentiments as themselves a kind of 'data' to which policy and politicians must respond.

Demos looks ahead to the next 20 years older and wiser. We may lack the spiky-haired idealism of our 1990s youth but we have not grown cynical. We are less overtly party political than in our middle phase but still have a focus of concern on the people in the bottom half of the income spectrum. (And throughout we have remained a very domestically-focused organisation, the internationalist intentions of the founding document left unrealised, notwithstanding the occasional venture into global analysis such as Robert Cooper's, reflected upon inside.)

Today we are equipped with a balanced portfolio of interests and expertise to continue making a difference in the British political and research conversation whether through our social policy concerns, such as the future of social care or what a contributory welfare system might look like; our work on social media and the fuzzy boundary between public and private in the Centre for the Analysis of Social Media; our new arrival Demos Finance with its mission to explain the complexities of the current debate about reforming finance to the concerned citizen; and my own special interest in the issues of minority integration and segregation in an open, liberal society. That should keep us busy for a while yet.

1 Demos – many successes but one big failure

Geoff Mulgan

Twenty years ago I and a band of collaborators set up Demos on a wing and prayer, and £5,000 in the bank. As so often, the main motive was frustration as much as idealism. The passions of the Thatcher period had run their course, as the limitations of her ideas had become more visible than the strengths. But Thatcher's hegemony was being superceded by a tired complacency, symbolised by the grey men who had summarily dispatched her to early retirement.

There was little sign of imagination in any of the parties. Society was changing in a multitude of ways, with a flood of new technologies, a maelstrom of change in everyday culture, and in the ethnic make-up of cities. But when we looked at the central institutions of society they appeared oblivious, barely touched by what was happening around them. The Thatcherites had at least had a refreshing lack of deference, even if in cultural terms they were rooted in old Britain, and often in the chauvinistic worst of old Britain. But the leaders of the early 1990s were staid, and relaxed in their relative lack of ambition.

So Demos tried to offer an alternative. Our diagnosis was quite simple – that politics had fallen behind. We argued that Britain was suffering from an over-centralisation of power in institutions which had lost trust, and didn't really deserve much of the trust that remained. We argued that democracy had to be about more than occasional elections between hierarchical political parties – and that the culture of democracy was relevant to every aspect of life. And we argued that politics needed to be invigorated by the most energetic parts of society, if it was to have much hope of dealing with the big issues, from inequality to climate change. Otherwise we were set for a long period when anti-politics would be the predominant mood.[1]

That spirit was summed up in the name we chose. Demos was about re-empowering the 'demos', about spreading power, and promoting the idea that democracy itself needed innovation: frozen in forms that made a great deal of sense in the 19th century it now risked becoming an anachronism. Above all we wanted to articulate an alternative to the hoarding habits of closed elites and share power.

That required attention to ideas – and to practice. In this respect we attempted to counterbalance the powerful literary influence on politics – which valued words over deeds, clever essays over workable ideas. This was (and still is) the dominant spirit of the political magazines, embodied in the style and choice of topics of figures like Christopher Hitchens, Ferdinand Mount and John Gray, and in the cultural studies tradition that had dominated *Marxism Today* (whose editor Martin Jacques was one of the Demos founders). At its best this tradition opens eyes and can be invigorating. But at its worst it encourages contempt for practical problem-solving.

So what happened? A twenty year period is hard to assess. It's too short to see the really long term trends, but too long to fit into everyday political punditry. At first glance the similarities between now and then jump out. Then as now a Conservative government which had previously had some ideas and energy, appeared becalmed. Then as now the UK was in the aftermath of a recession. Then as now there was pervasive distrust in power, and of a political world engrossed in often petty scandals, with Europe a running sore, obsessing the elites and the newspapers and annoying much of the public.

So if things are so similar today, surely Demos was a failure? By some measures the answer has to be yes, and as I'll argue later, within this broad failure there was a particularly large and more specific failure that we didn't spot at the time. No-one could claim that power has been radically redistributed or that British society has become markedly more open. We now know much more clearly than we did then that the 1980s and 1990s saw a hardening of social structures. The very period when newspapers like *The Sunday Times* were proclaiming a newly open and meritocratic age was in fact the opposite. Social mobility which increased for several decades after 1945 declined after 1979: the academic experts think that the policies of 1997–2010 revived it, but it's too soon to be certain.

Yet at the level of ideas and policies Demos was remarkably influential, probably more than we could have guessed. It helped that the only politician who attended its launch event went onto become Prime Minister for a decade, and was culturally in tune with the mix of activist social policy, communitarianism and openness in economics that we advocated.

One measure of success is the surprisingly high proportion of Demos topics and ideas that later appeared in other think-tank's work programmes a few years later. Many also adopted at least some of Demos' promiscuous approach – inviting politicians from the other side onto panels and seminars, and encouraging a freer and more fluid public conversation. The result is that today's Conservative-led government looks at times closer in spirit to Demos than Margaret Thatcher, particularly on issues like open data or neighbourhood empowerment. Some of key figures associated with Demos in its early days went on to fill prominent roles – Alan Duncan (author of its third publication) has been a senior minister in several departments, while Vince Cable (author of Demos's fourth publication) is Secretary of State for Business, Innovation and Skills. Former Director Tom Bentley was until recently in charge of policy in the Prime Minister's office in Australia. Many other staff also went onto influential roles – from Mark Leonard running the European Council on Foreign Relations to Ravi Gurumurthy in charge of government climate strategy, and Richard Reeves, chief adviser to the Deputy Prime Minister.

Some specific policies also made serious headway in government: from earned autonomy in local government to parental leave and consumer power in public services. Ideas about the machineries of government also bore fruit – in particular proposals for making government more horizontal, and joined up. For a time the UK was a pioneer – from units and budgets to targets and data – even if the momentum then passed to other countries in northern Europe and east Asia which took these ideas further (Whitehall still remains predominantly trapped in the vertical silos of 19th century administration).

More of Demos' ideas, however, were arguably too far ahead of the mainstream. Demos's first pamphlet of all proposed unitary taxation of multinationals – yet only in 2013 has this issue had even the slightest airing in national debate. The work done on behaviour change was undoubtedly pioneering in the mid 1990s – but there was almost no interest at the time, and it wasn't until 2010 that government set up the 'Behavioural Insights Team'. The same is true of the work on happiness, which predicted that this would become a key frame for public policy. Again, this did eventually happen – but in the mid-1990s there were few takers.

The ideas on how to innovate the big institutions – universities, civil service and so on – have scarcely dated, but nor have they been seriously contemplated. Ideas about using technology to transform democracy, including hybrids of direct and representative, are becoming real in countries such as Iceland, Estonia and Finland (in all of which Demos is well-known: indeed Finland has its own Demos). But the Mother of all Parliaments has by contrast preferred to stick with the tried and tested.

Demos arguably had more success with stories. We recognised that frames and narratives play as big a part in political change as individual stories, and, for better or worse, helped a lot of politicians to sharpen up their accounts. We were particularly interested in the story of Britain, and proposed an alternative take which had a big influence on government and its agencies, which Mark Leonard has revisited in this collection in Chapter 9. Some of the content was mocked (although Demos didn't actually use the much-pilloried phrase 'Cool Britannia'). But the overall argument was almost identical to the story of Britain portrayed at the

Olympics opening ceremony emphasising radicalism, innovation, and the democratic spirit of a multi-ethnic, outward looking nation. This account is now so much a conventional wisdom that it's hard to remember how fresh it was at a time when Britishness meant royalty and stately homes, and the ministry of culture was named the Department of Heritage.

This is perhaps another pointer to Demos' influence, which was about style as well as substance. Britain had many non-partisan institutions but these tended to be firmly rooted in the establishment, dedicated to dinners and seminars with a smattering of knights and lords careful not to stray too far from the middle ground. We hoped to combine freedom from party affiliation with an ethos that was radical, troublesome, and appealing to insurgents rather than incumbents. I enjoyed reminding guests at Demos 16th birthday party that the name is an anagram of 'sod'em' – and I believe that that spirit of demotic scepticism, allied to idealism, has been a vital strand in the best of our political traditions, albeit repeatedly worn down by proximity to power.

Yet for all the success in promoting ideas, ways of thinking, and specific policies, the bigger picture is one of frustration. Our aim in setting up Demos was to revitalise politics so that the majority – the 'demos' in its widest sense – would be reengaged with decisions. That mission failed (as Andrew Adonis explores in his essay).

There are many reasons – including the failure to reform the core institutions of democracy, beyond devolution, partial reform of the House of Lords and a few referendums on mayors. But one is that the changing class structure has transformed politics, and left significant parts of the 'demos' detached. Seen in the long view one of the most striking features of modern politics is the almost complete absence of organisations representing the relatively poor. The poorest quarter or fifth of the population have been disconnected and disempowered and are largely ignored by people in power. There are very few organisations dedicated to their interests, and most speak for them rather than representing them in a fuller sense.

There are plenty of people from poor backgrounds in parliament. But the vast majority have been through a university education. The result is that the interests of the top 10 per cent are vastly more visible and influential than the interests of a group that is numerically far greater. Read the leading newspapers and, even more than ever, they reflect the concerns of a small elite, mainly based in an arc that stretches across London from Kensington and Notting Hill to Islington. Things which happen in their circle are magnified; things outside tend to be ignored.

Yet this central fact of contemporary politics is of course oddly invisible, precisely because it's an absence: the things that aren't said, aren't argued, aren't fought for. It may be too soon to be definitive about why this shift has happened: to weigh up the relative impact of the decline of working class organisations during the 1980s; of notably poor leadership, particularly in the trade unions, over many years; of fractured interests. But there's no doubt of the scale of the change that has happened.

It's not to say that the poorest quarter don't have any voice. More than the rest they are the group most likely to be angered by immigration, or by Europe, or indeed by many other changes that symbolise their disempowerment. What's missing is any articulation of a programme, a coherent set of ideas that might represent their aspirations, their stake.

A handful of policies and many more projects and programmes are trying to counter these trends, amongst which my favourites include the Uprising programme training up young leaders in the big cities on how to gain and use power, and the studio schools (getting on for 50 open by 2014) that show just how much teenagers can be inspired to be active makers of the world around them. But these are relatively small scale, and in some respects are working against the grain of deeper trends.

So I'm disappointed that the core goal of opening power up hasn't been achieved. Less social mobility, a more closed political elite, and a more detached and anti-political 'demos', wasn't quite what we had in mind.

Notes

1 The book I published shortly after Demos' launch used this as its theme – with the title *Politics in an antipolitical age*.

2 From multiple intelligences to The Good Project

How theories of intelligence help to develop meaningful work

Howard Gardner

In the early 1980s, when I published my theory of multiple intelligences, I received the Warholian fifteen minutes of fame. At the time, I was a psychologist working both with children and with brain-damaged adults; and I thought that 'MI theory' would be responded to chiefly by other psychologists. As it turned out, the theory was and has remained of much more interest to educators than to psychologists, and, according to the principle enunciated above, I began to direct increasing energy to understanding the education of young people.

My essay for Demos in the mid-1990s captured that period well. I was already concerned that 'accountability' pressures in the United States (and in Britain) would push for simple, short answer, often multiple choice kinds of assessments. While such instruments are inexpensive and produce easy-to-compare results, they almost always undervalue deeper forms of thinking and understanding, which do not lend themselves to quick-and-dirty assessments.

And so in my essay, I made the case for inculcating deeper forms of understanding, upon which we can draw to make sense of issues and problems that we have not already encountered in textbooks or lectures. At the conclusion of the essay, I sketched a few ways in which MI theory might help both to teach for understanding and to assess the extent to which students have achieved genuine and generative understandings.

I continue to be concerned with issues of education and, indeed, if anything, the landscape of pre-tertiary education looks even bleaker in the United States than it did twenty years go.

Dating back to 1989, when then President George H. W. Bush and then Governor Bill Clinton convened an education conference in Charlottesville, Virginia, there has in effect been a single educational policy in the United States. I can be succinct: the admirable goals set out almost 25 years ago have not been achieved, and in my view the current educational policies will not move us closer to their achievement.

But my own scholarly work has moved in quite a different direction, one that is quite consonant with the Demos agenda, but one that I could not have anticipated twenty years ago. With long-time colleagues William Damon and Mihaly Csikszentmihalyi, and a cohort of wonderful researchers at Harvard led by Lynn Barendsen, Wendy Fischman, and Carrie James, I have been studying the nature of 'good work'. Moreover, under the GoodWork banner, we have over time launched a number of cognate projects, going by names like Good Play, Good Collaboration, Good Citizenship, Good Life, which we have now aggregated under the header The Good Project (thegoodproject.org) In what follows, I characterise briefly the nature and goals of this effort.

There are plenty of reasons to decry contemporary society. Though the world as a whole is richer than it has been in the past, the inequities within most societies are great and, all too often, growing. New technologies have exciting potential, but all too often they are used simply to promote products or to confirm already established attitudes and practices. Democratic ideals are promulgated universally, but are honored more in the breach than in the practice, even in societies where democratic processes are well established. And the most pressing problems in the world – devastating diseases, global warming, violent ethnic clashes – are typically ignored or pushed to the side, rather than addressed frontally and competently.

Against this depressing background, it is more important than ever to identify and to understand those individuals, institutions, and professions that merit admiration, and that are worthy of emulation. This is the research goal of the Good

Project. And having established some of the marks of good work, it is crucial to support those individuals, institutions, and professions that want to achieve, enact good work. That is the practical goal of the Good Project.

Launched in the mid-1990s with a study of major professions; the GoodWork Project serves as a model for describing what we are trying to achieve. Over the course of a decade, my colleagues and I conducted in-depth interviews with over 1200 professionals in nine professions, ranging from medicine and law to journalism and philanthropy. On the basis of these interviews, we identified the three crucial ingredients of good work: technical Excellence, personal Engagement, and Ethical practices – what we call the 'three Es', or, somewhat whimsically, ENA.

Acting as researchers, we could say that at this point in our studies, our job was largely done. But we were spurred by an unexpected finding among young participants in our study. These workers, in their late teens, twenties, and early thirties, repeatedly told us that they admired good work, they wanted to do it, and some day they intended to practice and embody it.

Yet too many of them told us that they could not *afford* to do good work at this early point in their working life. That is because, in their view, their peers were cutting corners and they were not going to cede their chance of fame and success by being 'holier' than others. In effect, they told us: 'Good work is for later – for now let us cut corners, let us compromise.'

Deeply troubled by this state of affairs in the United States, we decided to become directly involved with young people. And so over the next few years, we began to develop courses – full term and briefer – in which we familiarised young people with the issues and choices involved in good work. We also developed a set of materials, called The Good Work Toolkit. This compendium exposed young persons to the kinds of dilemmas faced by workers in different fields and helped them to think through possible courses of actions and to anticipate their probable consequences. Both the courses that we mounted and the toolkit that we developed have now been used in multiple settings both in the United States and abroad. We are well into the process of assessing the effectiveness of this instrument.

It is worth mentioning other dividends of both the GoodWork Project and The Good Project. These range from a travelling curriculum that is used in journalism, to training future ethical leaders in a network of schools in India, to occasional seminars and conferences across a range of professions, including an international conference on GoodWork convened by our research group in March of 2013. We have had numerous connections to the positive psychology movement in the UK and recently we have joined forces with colleagues there, whose 'Action for Happiness' initiative shares many of the goals of our undertaking.

If changing the educational system in the US poses a significant challenge, establishing an atmosphere of good work, good citizenship, and other 'goods' is even more formidable. It is even more important. I have found it personally satisfying to understand the nature of intelligence, creativity, and leadership. But if in the end, intellect, creativity, and leadership are turned to selfish or even destructive ends, that is lamentable. The overarching goal of the Good Project, and of my own recent writing and action, is to help increase the likelihood that individuals and institutions will use their talents to advance the wider good of the demos, the people.

3 Sharper Vision, in retrospect

The BBC and the communications revolution

Ian Hargreaves

One of the very first Demos publications, written in 1993, was my ambitious attempt to think through the implications of digital technology on the UK's most important media organisation: the BBC. The convergence of broadcast, satellite and cable platforms was already plain, but the emergence of the commercial internet was at an early stage.

Today, with James Purnell, a former Labour cabinet minister, newly installed as the corporation's Director of Digital Strategy and the recent embarrassment of a £100m back-office information technology write-off, the subject remains highly salient. Just what are we entitled to expect of the BBC in a digital world dominated by Google, Apple, Amazon and Facebook?

The motivation of Demos Paper 5 (*Sharper Vision: the BBC and the communications revolution*) was to make sense of my own conflicting emotions and thoughts following a stint inside the BBC in the late 1980s. How to develop the BBC to its maximum potential, without squashing everything in its path and so diminishing the overall broadcast ecology? How to protect against the organisation's tendency to bureaucratic isolation? The technology context looked promising, compared with the predictable dullness of a duopoly settlement with ITV which had dominated the spectrum-constrained UK broadcasting landscape since the 1960s.

In the pamphlet, I got one big thing right and one wrong. My error was to assume that the licence fee could not survive in a more complex and jostling media ecology, where mobile phones would turn into televisions. The BBC, therefore, should be encouraged towards a mixed funding base and an ownership structure which reflected the direct interests of viewers and listeners rather than the financial control which inevitably arises when ministers hold the purse strings.

A version of this bolder constitutional thinking about the ownership of the BBC may yet have its day, but I would say that the great diversity of the internet makes a centralised and politically determined form of funding like the licence fee more attractive because its uniqueness in a digital world provides such diversity of competitive forms for the BBC. (I am just a little to tempted to predict here that the licence fee will remain at the core of the BBC's funding, confident that this will be enough to ensure its demise.)

What the pamphlet did spot was the emergence of BSkyB as the new defining broadcast competitor for the BBC, based upon a Pay TV business model. A hybrid of Rupert Murdoch's Sky and the supposedly better bred British Satellite Broadcasting, it was not wholly obvious in 1993 that Murdoch's days of demanding the privatisation or dismemberment of the BBC (a favourite sport during the Thatcher premiership) were done. In truth, by the 1990s, the BBC was Athens to Murdoch's Rome; a useful point of reference in a high-stakes commercial game. In effect, a new-wave duopoly, albeit set in a more complex ecology in which both giants would be challenged by the internet.

From an industrial policy perspective, the 1993 landscape left much to be desired: 'an ITV system characterised by small regional monopolies, an unsustainable regulatory muddle in the satellite sector and a cable sector dominated by non-UK interests.' The pamphlet asked: how can we enable the BBC to be a more significant and ambitious player on the world stage; or, as I might put it today, a flagship for the UK creative economy? I wrote:

Here is a sharper vision of the BBC's future: a BBC liberated from political control, free to invest, to expand and to make alliances and to develop new services. Such a BBC would have a first rate chance to emerge as a major UK player in the international media marketplace.

In the event, it was Channel 4 which blazed a trail in providing markets for a new breed of independent TV production companies; speech radio never flourished far away from the BBC mothership and successive leaders of the BBC struggled to reconcile commercial ambition overseas with dedicated public service at home. There was a cost to the persistent conservativism of policy.

Yet it has also to be acknowledged that one big reason that such radical talk never made it out of 'think-tank land' was that the BBC, for all its self-inflicted dramas, from the Hutton Inquiry to Savile's paedophilia, maintained reassuring quality and the loyalty of its audience, especially the super-served demographic that can't live without Radio 4. After the unruly talk of the Thatcher years, the governments of Major, Blair, Brown and Cameron-Clegg have been happy to let the old BBC Routemaster roll along the road, even if for a while Alastair Campbell was hanging off the back platform screaming about something or other.

It would be a mistake to assume that this Summer Holiday approach will do indefinitely. Today, with a fecund internet throwing up new media platforms on all sides, the BBC does not have (as it did in its first century) a problem of being the biggest kid in the playground. Its problem is to uncover new forms of value: to ensure that its relevance and reputation grow. Today, the BBC's reach and cultural significance is challenged, not only by rival media groups, but by digital companies like Google. If cable and satellite were a wake-up call for a duopolistic BBC, the internet is an always-on warning siren. How should the BBC respond?

Today, I would not press the cause of mutualisation and, personally, I am content to support the licence fee so long as my fellow citizens will agree to pay it. What we should expect from the BBC is a more imaginative and determined approach to the internet, based upon the application of its public service values to the provision of a platform or platforms for content of many types.

This needs to go far beyond the one-week catch-up offered by the iPlayer. There is an opening to provide access to audience for a potentially vast array of new creators; an opportunity to curate this in new ways and a way of enriching the gene pool of a global platform system otherwise shaped essentially by competition between the commercial business models and voluntary approaches to ethics of a handful of American firms.

A good starting point already exists inside the BBC. It is called Digital Public Space and its first thought (a sound one) is to liberate the BBC's vast and invaluable archive, which is today imprisoned in the corporation's vault because it is too time-consuming, expensive and an insufficiently high corporate priority, to make it available, whether to those who have already paid for it or to those who would be willing to pay to make use of it.

This takes the BBC into the fray on re-designing copyright, which is being torn out of shape by the competing forces of anxious rights owners on one side and confused consumers on the other. The BBC is probably the only organisation big and potentially imaginative enough to define a new public interest dimension here, which could have the effect of greatly enriching the UK's cultural life, as well as opening up the BBC vaults, as the current Government's reforms intend to do for the licensing of 'orphan works'. All of this is vaguely in line with the ambitions of other big international initiatives, such as the EU's Europeana project and with the important digital copyright licensing hub currently under development in the UK.

In short, the BBC needs to be able to recover its ability to think new and think big, whilst at the same time keeping the old bus on the road, calling at familiar stops in a reassuring manner.

4 Vote early, vote often

Going back to the ballot box

Andrew Adonis and Adam Tyndall

Back to Greece: the scope for direct democracy by Andrew Adonis and Demos's first director Geoff Mulgan was one of the organisation's first pamphlets on the political process itself. It diagnosed an ailing democracy. Twenty years later, the patient hasn't recovered – perhaps because the original diagnosis was, in retrospect, fundamentally mistaken. Instead of idealistic new forms of participation, the priority should be practical reforms to strengthen the basic foundation of democracy: the mass franchise.

What was written back then is substantially true today:

Modern government is exclusive and elitist. It... encourages political elites to trade simplistic, cut-and-dried solutions to problems as the currency of electoral politics. Political alienation and ignorance are systemic. But neither feature is new to the 1980s or 1990s, however stark they seem today. They have gone hand-in-hand with representative government; only their form, and the capacity to do anything to overcome them, have changed over the decades.[1]

In key respects, the patient has deteriorated. Voter engagement has been far lower post-1994 than it was pre-1994. In the 14 UK general elections between 1945 and 1992, the average turnout was 77 per cent.[2] In 2001, turnout dropped below 60 per cent for the first time and in 2010 was still below two-thirds of the electorate. In the 4 general elections between 1997 and 2010, turnout averaged 64 per cent.

This 13-point drop in turnout between 1992 and 2010 has not been uniformly distributed across the electorate. What is most striking are the huge increases in the turnout gaps between different demographic groups. For example, the gap between AB turnout (managers and professionals) and DE turnout (unskilled and manual workers) has increased from 6 points in 1992 to 19 points in 2010.

As for age, whilst the turnout among over 65s has dropped from 83 per cent to 76 per cent, among 18-24 year olds it has fallen from 63 per cent to just 44 per cent. The 'age gap' of 20 points has become a 32-point chasm and there seems no prospect of recovery in the near future. The Hansard Society reports that, in 2013, 'just 12 per cent of 18-24 year olds now say they are certain to vote. This is a 10 percentage point fall in the last year, and a decline from the 30 per cent recorded in [2011].'[3] This compares with 59 per cent (down from 72 per cent two years ago) of over-55s reporting that they are certain to vote in a general election. No wonder cuts in pensioner benefits are off the table whilst young people are increasingly expected to pick up the tab.

Turnout in local elections, which has always been lower than in general elections, has also declined. Average turnout in the 1940s was 45 per cent. In the 1980s it was still above 40 per cent. In the 2000s it fell to 36 per cent and in 2012 it dropped below a third of the electorate to just 31 per cent. Young adults barely vote or engage in local politics and there are very few young councillors. In 2012, Leeds had more councillors over the age of 75 than under the age of 35.

Mistaken diagnosis

The 1994 Adonis/Mulgan diagnosis was partly rooted in rational choice theory. James Fishkin[4] and Anthony Downs[5] were cited for their work on the 'rational ignorance' of ordinary citizens. Voters have no reason to find out about issues if their opinion will never be asked for. Downs went as far as to say that it is largely irrational to vote at all given the high costs – registration, travel, time etc – and the low probability of one's vote making a difference to the result.

Yet most of the adult population does vote in general elections. This is what Morris Fiorina called 'the paradox that ate rational choice theory.'[6] As James Fowler puts it:

Unless we assume collateral benefits like the rewarding feeling of doing one's civic duty, rational choice models yield predictions that are at odds with the reality that millions of people vote in large elections... [and] a substantial literature that indicates most people are habitual voters.[7]

Back to Greece simply took it for granted that general election turnout in excess of 70 per cent would continue. Rather than tackle the fundamentals of voter engagement in existing national and local elections, the Adonis/Mulgan recommendations on 'informed participation' sought to move up the escalator of democratic participation. In retrospect this was overambitious. There were three specific suggestions:

Voter Juries

'These national juries – perhaps held once or twice a year – would examine issues of major public interest or controversy... Each jury would consist of about 20 randomly selected adults. Each would last for one week with the aim or reaching verdicts on specific questions raised by the issues under consideration. Their verdicts would have no constitutional force, although we would expect them – and summaries of their discussions – to attract wide public attention.'[8]

Voter Vetoes

'The Voter Veto would introduce the advisory referendum into Britain for use in the specific case of legislation passed by parliament, or a decision made by a local council. At national level, if 1m voters – more than 2 per cent of the electorate – signed a petition for a referendum to be called, a poll would be held on the issue on the local election day in May following, and the legislation – or decision – would not be implemented pending the result. The outcome of the referendums would be advisory; parliament and councils would be free to refuse to modify their earlier decisions in the face of an adverse referendum majority if they so resolved, provided they formally considered the result before so doing.'[9]

Voter Feedback

'Our third suggestion is to draw on the many experiences from around the world in using new electronic communications to engage citizens in decisions.'[10]

It is obviously essential to deploy new social and communications media to the cause of politics and government. The proliferation of media and – crucially – user-generated content has revolutionised traditional media industries and (to a lesser extent) the ways in which the electorate participate in democratic debate. But the shortcomings of the other two recommendations are stark in hindsight.

The idea that a state-led television series called 'Voter Juries' would get more than a handful of viewers, and command any special legitimacy, is risible. As for referendums, if basic voter turnout in general and local elections is so low, it is hard to argue that the solution is yet more voting with ever diminishing turnout. Furthermore, the 2 per cent hurdle virtually guarantees that many referendum issues – national and local – would be of passionate concern to only a tiny minority of the electorate.

'Back to Greece' also recognised that 'until cable and other technologies reach near-100 per cent penetration they will not be legitimate as voting mechanisms.'[11] Two decades on, they still haven't. Even the greater use of postal voting has given rise to increased concern about fraud.

Vote early, vote often

The key imperative for democratic reformers should therefore be to reinvigorate the mass franchise and stimulate greater turnout in national and local elections. Without this representative democracy could start to lose its legitimacy. It is vital that voting starts young, both to represent the young and also to instil the 'voting habit'.

There is a significant body of academic evidence to show that casting one's ballot on election day is habitual. As Donald Green and Ron Shachar put it:

If two people whose psychological propensities to vote are identical should happen to make different choices about whether to go to the polls on election day, these behaviours will alter their likelihoods of voting in the next election. In other words, holding pre-existing individual and environmental attributes constant, merely going to the polls increases one's chance of returning.[12]

Another study by Kevin Denny and Orla Doyle, concludes that 'voting in one election increases the probability of voting in a subsequent election by 13 per cent.'[13] This number is brought down from an astonishing 26 per cent on the basis that some of their sample will have established a habit before the start of their data set and that 'it is critical that one allows for the fact that politicization starts before the voting age and has long-lasting consequences for political behaviour.'[14] This suggests that the earliest voting choices have the biggest impact.

First time voting by teenagers and young adults is clearly critical to habit formation thereafter. The question is how to get young people to vote in far larger numbers. A combination of citizenship education, a voting age reduced to 16, and locating the first vote in a young person's school or college seem the most promising options.

Not 'back to Greece' but 'back to the ballot box'

Eric Plutzer writes of the voting habit:

As young citizens confront their first election, all of the costs of voting are magnified: they have never gone through the process of registration, may not know the location of their polling place, and may not have yet developed an understanding of party differences and key issues. Moreover, their peer group consists almost entirely of other non-voters: their friends cannot assure them that voting has been easy, enjoyable, or satisfying. Young people also lack many of the resources that can promote participation. Because they have little disposable income, they are not attractive targets for parties seeking campaign contributions or for interest groups mounting direct mail campaigns. Few of them own homes, have stakes in community politics, or have completed college. Thus it is not surprising that… their turnout is relatively low.[15]

Votes at 16; students registered by and at their place of study; a polling booth in every school, college and university; preparation for voting being a key part of citizenship education – these simple reforms address most of Plutzer's points. If they were implemented, virtually all 16–18 year olds, and about half of all 18 to 22 year olds (i.e. those at university or full-time college), would be registered at their place of study and cast their first votes there. Voting en masse would reduce many of the psychological barriers for young people approaching their first vote. It would be a group activity for young people and an expectation within their educational institution. Citizenship education (introduced into English schools in 2002) would then lead naturally to voting; mock elections would lead to real elections, just as mock exams lead to real exams; and local candidates and parties would treat schools, and their voters, with a degree of attention and seriousness largely lacking at present.

These reforms should apply not only for national elections but also for local elections, where the issues (such as local transport and amenities) are of vital concern to young people. They would also encourage the political parties to recruit more young members, and to stand young candidates – including students – for council elections in particular.

Green and Shachar conclude that if you manage to 'lure someone to the voting booth, and you will raise his or her propensity to vote in a future election.'[16] Better still, bring the voting booth to the voter.

As for citizenship education, developmental psychologist Judith Torney-Purta, states that:

Schools achieve the best results in fostering civic engagement when they rigorously teach civic content and skills, ensure an open classroom climate for discussing issues, emphasize the importance of the electoral process, and encourage a participative school culture.[17]

What better way to achieve this than to do it for real, with a vote at the end of the process?

England's elite have always understood the importance of starting young. When Old Etonian, Jesse Norman, was asked why David Cameron was surrounded in his Government by so many other Old Etonians, he replied:

Other schools don't have the same commitment to public service. They do other things. It's one of the few schools where the pupils really do run vast chunks of the school themselves. So they don't defer in quite the same way, they do think there's the possibility of making change through their own actions... Things like rhetoric and poetry and public speaking and performance are incredibly important to young people succeeding in life.

Indeed so. The imperative is not 'back to Greece' but 'back to the ballot box'.

Notes

1 Andrew Adonis and Geoff Mulgan, *Back to Greece: the scope for direct democracy*, Demos 3, 1994, p 2.

2 All election statistics from Ipsos-Mori's 'How Britain Voted' research and/or Colin Rallings and Michael Thrasher, *British Electoral Facts 1832 – 2012,* Biteback, 2012.

3 The Hansard Society, *Audit of Political Engagement 10: The 2013 Report,* Hansard Society, 2013, p 36.

4 James S. Fishkin, *The Voice of the People: Public Opinion andDemocracy,* Yale University Press, 1995.

5 Anthony Downs, *An Economic Theory of Democracy,* Harper & Brothers, 1957.

6 Morris Fiorina, *Information and Rationality in Elections,* in Information and Democratic Processes, John Ferejohn and James Kuklinski, eds., University of Illinois Press, 1990.

7 James H. Fowler, *Habitual Voting and Behavioral Turnout,* The Journal of Politics 68:2, 2006, p 33.

8 Andrew Adonis and Geoff Mulgan, *Back to Greece: the scope for direct democracy*, Demos 3, 1994, p 22.

9 Ibid, p 23.

10 Ibid, p 24.

11 Ibid, p 19.

12 Donald P Green and Ron Shachar, *Habit Formation and Political Behaviour: Evidence of Consuetude in Voter Turnout,* British Journal of Political Science 30:4, 2000, p 562.

13 Kevin Denny and Orla Doyle, *Does Voting History Matter? Analysing Persistence in Turnout,* American Journal of Political Science, 53:1, 2009, p 17.

14 Ibid, p 31.

15 Eric Plutzer, *Becoming a Habitual Voter: Inertia, Resources, and Growth in Youth Adulthood,* The American Political Science Review 96:1, 2002, p 42.

16 Donald P Green and Ron Shachar, Habit Formation and Political Behaviour: Evidence of Consuetude in Voter Turnout, British Journal of Political Science 30:4, 2000, p 562.

17 Judith Torney-Purta, The School's Role in Developing Civic Engagement: A study of Adolescents in Twenty-Eight Countries, Applied Developmental Science, 6, 2002, p 203.

5 Auditing: the explosion goes on

Audit is inadequate because it can only count certain things

Michael Power

In 1993 the late Anthony Hopwood, then professor of international accounting at LSE, introduced me to Geoff Mulgan, founding Director of Demos. I had written a draft paper entitled 'The Audit Society' which had been presented to a small group of academics in what was called 'the History of the Present' workshop. The observable expansion of audit in Britain seemed to me to be systematic and significant in a way that no one had yet addressed. Audit was becoming an entire style of governing, hence the appeal of my paper to the Foucauldians of the workshop.

I recall trying to draft the new document with the 'intelligent layman' in mind. Mulgan and his colleagues wanted more persuasive evidence for the so-called explosion of auditing, which I did not have and needed to find. The first paragraph of the essay provides a list of the many different audits that existed at that time. The more I looked for these 'audit' labels, the more I found. The sheer reach of the idea of audit, even if all these different practices were varied in some way, was actually a big surprise. It also explains why *The Audit Explosion* was itself so successful – professionals and academics of many different kinds could recognise something from their own worlds.

There were six basic overlapping elements to the original argument which still remain plausible two decades later. First I challenged the idea that audits are neutral in their operation. Rather, they shape conceptions of accountability and channel the efforts of different actors, making them pay increasing attention to the measurable and auditable aspects of performance even as they know that such measures tell only partial stories of real performance. This was central to a change in UK public management and beyond – the so-called new public management.

Second, the audit explosion represented not just the expansion of a technical practice but also constituted a new form of government. Today we might call this form of government 'neoliberal' in the sense of seeking to intervene in public organisations indirectly via disciplines such as accountancy and audit, and acting on internal structures to stimulate self-regulation and self-management.

At the centre of this indirect form of government is the third theme of the audit explosion: control of control. Indirect government necessitates the use of systems of internal control for regulatory and evaluatory purposes. This in turn requires such systems to be visible and capable of being evaluated. However, auditable control systems were too easily identified with the substance of performance itself. For example, teaching and medical quality came to be thought of as aspects of systems rather than products of individual expertise.

Fourth, many of these changes were motivated by ideals of transparency that are impossible to realise. The assumption was that transparency would stimulate desired behaviour modification as practitioners were required to give public accounts of performance. The private life of the professions was to be made more public and audit was one of the key mechanisms by which this would happen. Yet as plausible as such ideals sounded – who could be against transparency? – they failed to acknowledge something long-recognised by accounting scholars. The transparency ideal is always moderated and mediated by specific practices of accounting and auditing. These forms of accounting for performance are not a 'clear window' into an organisation but are themselves partial representations. Indeed, this partiality is the source of the power of accounting. Some activities in an organisation may be made visible, significant and comparable via accounting while others become invisible, idiosyncractic and incomparable. There is no pure accounting as such.

The fifth theme is that regulation, accounting and audit are in a constant process of failure and reform which is even more obvious in the financially stressed world of 2013. The audit explosion was for this reason paradoxical since the necessary failure of audit to realise the dreams of control resulted in ever more intense investments in audit. It is a sense of this inherent failure that may have driven the 'nudge' initiative in government policy making. On the one hand the idea speaks optimistically to the need to work with the grain of human and organisational behaviours. On the other hand it also reflects political disdain for the possibility of successful 'big' intervention.

The sixth theme tries to identify the engine of the audit explosion. In 1994 it was suggested that we live in an age of increasing evidence-based demands on organisational performance. There was, and is, a deep-seated cultural imperative to transform organisations so that they can be checked, evaluated and audited. For some, this is the phenomenon of 'red tape' and 'box-ticking'. For others it is a product of adversarial blame cultures. Yet today, despite these critiques, the ideal of 'don't tell me, show me' has been normalised and is as strong as ever.

The Audit Explosion and the academic books and papers which were developed from it are far from perfect. There have been numerous critiques addressing such matters as the analytical and empirical vagueness of the concept of audit, my reliance on secondary sources, the UK-centric nature of the story and a tendency to sample on the dependent variable – audit – without exploring underlying drivers and institutional variation. There is a lot of truth in these criticisms. Yet the reach of both *The Audit Explosion* and a follow-on monograph – *The Audit Society* – suggests some success in naming a phenomenon of central concern to scholars and practitioners across many different fields.

Indeed, despite the UK-centrism, the reception in other European countries, such as Sweden, has also been significant although the arguments have travelled less well to the United States. Overall, I firmly believe that 'disciplined exaggeration' is necessary to generate real insight. The benefits can sometimes outweigh the apparent scholarly flaws. Indeed most significant advances in intellectual and practical fields are of this nature.

The Audit Explosion circulated widely in policy circles and yet did little to turn the tide of audit. In 1994 it could be read as a post-Thatcher critique but in fact audit and evaluation as instruments of government accelerated under New Labour. They were attractive methods of central control over distant entities. Yet the mid to late 1990s brought another twist in the evolution of the audit society. Following the BSE crisis and other failures in public and private services, risk and risk management became a new focus of attention in UK government and elsewhere.

The risk of public censure and reputational damage was dramatised by the experience of Shell when it disposed of the Brent Spar in the North sea in 1995. The power of media and the mobilisation of German public opinion against Shell heralded a new kind of risk for organisations. Scholars have described this risk variously as 'secondary' risk, 'institutional' risk, and the 'disaster after the disaster'. They commonly point to an operating environment in which all organisations must be mindful of threat of adverse opinion about their activities. This applies as much to government agencies and regulators as to private corporations. Today this risk is amplified by various forms of social media.

In 2004 I argued in the *Risk Management of Everything* that this expansion of risk discourse had little to do with society becoming more dangerous – other than in the reputational sense outlined above – and was really a continuation of the audit society by other means. Risk management has become the language of accountability and being able to demonstrate conformity to institutionalised risk management principles is now a way of demonstrating legitimacy to regulators, publics and others. Today conceptions of good corporate governance and risk management are almost indistinguishable from each other.

And yet Enron collapsed in 2002 with a perfectly demonstrable Enterprise Risk Management System. To take a more recent example the Mid-Staffordshire NHS trust report in 2013 shows how it pursued targets relating to risk to patients at the expense of patients themselves. And in 2007 financial regulators focused on easily auditable risk management systems for individual banks without looking at the aggregate systemic weaknesses this created. There is a wide consensus among regulators and regulated alike that tick-box risk management is bad. Yet these forms of practice persist. Why?

I have been thinking about this question for over two decades. Most recently, I have tried to refine the focus on the mechanism of the audit explosion, namely the creation and expansion of 'audit trails' inside organisations which link the actions of individuals to performance reporting requirements. Much more work remains to be done but it seems to me that Coase's famous theory of organisations as a 'nexus of contracts' needs to be updated.

Modern organisations in both public and private sectors have become a *nexus of audit trails*. Organisations are constituted by webs of practices to provide evidence of performance which may be more or less dense. These practices are deeply ingrained in organisational life and hard to shift or change. This may be a somewhat pessimistic view but it seems better to begin to confront this reality than to imagine that a one-off campaign to reduce red tape and bureaucracy will ever be effective.

Both *The Audit Explosion* and *The Risk Management of Everything* were essentially prolegomena to larger academic works but they have had, and continue to have, a public life of their own. Demos gave me the freedom to explore popular versions of arguments and to build an intellectual architecture for later work. Indeed, it is no exaggeration to say that my entire academic and advisory career hinged on the opportunity given to me by Demos in 1994.

6 Reflections on the post-modern state

International relations after the Cold War

Robert Cooper

My Demos essay *The post-modern state and the world order* was a product of the four years I spent as Head of the Policy Planning Staff in the Foreign Office. I took up this post on 1 January 1989 thinking I might be the wrong person because 'I knew nothing about East–West relations or nuclear weapons'. It didn't matter because in the following four years the world was turned upside down. The essay was an attempt to understand the changes that were going on, and are still going on today. It brought together a number of puzzles.

First, there was the end of the Cold War itself: not so much why it ended, as how it ended. I found the CFE Treaty (on conventional forces in Europe) a particular puzzle. It was contrary to all strategic logic that enemies should allow challenge inspection of their military equipment. How did this, and indeed the whole category of confidence building measures fit into our normal foreign policy assumptions? Answer: they didn't.

Second were the two wars that marked this period. The first was Gulf War I. Like all successful wars, afterwards it seems obvious that we should have fought; but at the time George Bush (and I) hesitated; Margaret Thatcher (and Simon Fraser – then my deputy) did not. The latter remarked that if we were going to make a reality of a new world order we had to fight. This phrase was later used by the President himself. It is also worth remembering that the vote in the US Senate was a very close-run thing.

The second war was that in the Balkans. Here, we had more time to think but we still did not know what to think. In retrospect it is clear that we should have intervened much earlier, and with the threat or the use of force. But I'm still not sure what the principle behind this should have been. In the case of Saddam Hussein's invasion of Kuwait we had two possible principles: the idealist UN principle about not invading sovereign territories, or the realist principle that we had to defend balance/pluralism in the Gulf, an area of vital interest because of its oil. In the Balkans it was not clear that either of these principles were engaged.

The Balkan wars were civil wars so the principle from the UN Charter was the one of non-intervention. (I remember someone, ridiculously, arguing for recognition of Bosnia on the grounds that this would make it an inter-state war, allowing us to intervene.) Nor was it clear that our interests were engaged: there were refugees, but the cost of either accommodating keeping them out was going to be less than the cost of intervention; the risk of spill-over seemed minimal. That a humanitarian tragedy was in process was visible every night on TV, and so we sent humanitarian expeditions – and that was the wrong response.

In the end the principles formulated by Tony Blair in his Chicago speech are not a bad set of yardsticks for considering intervention; but every case is particular. These are not the whole answer either. For Europe, the Balkan crisis was in some way an intellectual crisis: Britain, France and Germany all reacted in different ways. In the end it was probably the French who were closest to be being right.

Whereas in 1914 a Balkan crisis was an occasion for the great powers to compete for territory in the 1990s everyone was looking for excuses to stay out. A remark by Prof Lawrence Freedman – that during the Cold War policy makers failed to understand that two things were going on simultaneously: the Cold War and anti-imperialist wars of liberation – has stuck in my head since. The 20th-century was the century of decolonisation: this impacted not just on the colonies but also on the would-be imperial powers. Hence the birth of the pre-modern: the ungoverned territory ripe for colonisation but, in the absence of imperial powers, left to rot.

Finally, there was the puzzle of the European Union. Both the glory and the liberty of Europe came out of competition among small states; but the destruction of Europe has come from the same competition – when it took the form of war. It is obvious that the peace and prosperity with which the European Union is associated are something to be proud of. But the idea of a European super state also looked like a mistake.

This was not just nostalgia for the traditions of Europe but came from a Thatcherite preference for competition, and also from a feeling that small states are better governed than big ones. Both the idea of a single European state and the idea of fully separate independent sovereign states seemed unsatisfactory. I recall being irritated by hearing a Chinese diplomat going on about noninterference in internal affairs, and I probably lectured him to the effect that all progress came precisely through such interference. Somewhere, out of this and out of the CFE Treaty came the idea of the post-modern.

Twenty years later – the essay was based on a talk I gave in 1993 – how do these ideas stand up? The answer is, not badly. I described a taxonomy of states: the pre-modern still struggling towards functioning states in parts of the developing world; the modern, including most of the big powers – the US, China and so on; the post-modern, in particular the countries of the European Union which have benefitted from less rather than more national sovereignty.

I exaggerated in each of the three cases: the pre-modern has not spread so fast, nor proved as much of a danger as I suggested. In fact it is striking how, in places like Somalia and Lebanon, the pull of order and civilisation, remains remarkably strong. There is an awful lot of ruin in a state and the urge to preserve or reconstruct order is very strong. The average person does not want a revolution. And I was overoptimistic about the post-modern. The idea of the nation state remains strong and even in the most post-modern countries people find it hard to imagine anything else. Did I over-emphasise the CFE Treaty? We seem to be getting on without it. My own inclination would have been to have tried harder to construct a lasting open (post-modern) relationship with Russia. At one point my slogan was: 'Enlarge the integrated military structure, not the Alliance'. No doubt this would have failed: Russia had not changed in the way that Europe had; and it would have been politically impossible to have refused Article V guarantees to countries such as Poland. But I still think a real working CFE Treaty is something we should still try to reconstruct.

And, as for the modern, I laid too much stress on the predatory nature of the state. Modern states are all different: China is dynamic, possibly nationalist; India is sleepy but can also be roused to nationalism; Brazil has traditions different from both. Perhaps I should have said more about the conditions which make states dangerous: the moment of rapid industrialisation, the beginnings of democracy. Finally, I should have underlined that these were ideal types and the USA, for example, is post-modern in its relationship with Canada, modern in its relationship with China – and pre-modern in its policies on gun control.

This is still not a bad map of the political geography of the world. The problem is that maps are helpful; but they do not tell you where you should want to go.

It is striking today still how little sense of direction there is in foreign policy anywhere. The United States seems to be tinkering with old problems like arms control and the Middle East peace process, but without new convictions or conceptions – and drone strikes are not a substitute for either. China seems caught between its sensible concept of 'Peaceful Rise' and its need to please the nationalist populism that the regime itself fosters.[1] Indeed the mystery is whether China has anything that could be called foreign policy at all – seeing that there is no one responsible for foreign affairs in the Politburo. Russia is turning in on itself, trying to isolate itself from anything outside the control of its government – which means the rest of the world. Japan's leadership is retreating into the past and the US alliance. The EU perhaps knows what it wants but lacks conviction in vision, coherence in policy and organisation.

Thus, twenty years after the end of the Cold War we still do not know where we want to go. In the past there was always some general conception of foreign policy. In European history this normally had to do with balance, though there were occasional bursts of belief in cooperation – the Concert of Europe, the League of Nations etc. Today both editorial writers and policymakers cling to old concepts and old problems. There is some danger in this. In the first Gulf War we made the right decision because we had the right frame of reference. In Bosnia we did not know what to think and failed to act. For the second Gulf War action was taken again without a strategic framework, with disastrous consequences.

My original title for the essay was: 'Is There A New World Order?' The implied answer to this question was: 'No'. With the end of the fixed framework Cold War we had no yardstick against which to measure our options or actions. Such an order can be created only piece by piece; but if we have some idea of where we want to go that would provide guidance for action.

In today's world there should be no doubt about our objectives. We live in a complex world of international markets and international interdependence. It is made more complex because it has more actors, because they are sometimes new to power and to world politics and because of their history and culture is different from our own. Nevertheless because of its interdependence, this is a world in which conflict is now expensive. In the longer run the costs of failing to cooperate, for example over climate change, will be even higher. This is a highly organised world in every area except politics. We need, as the European Union has done, to turn interdependence into an advantage. In the end – and this is a very distant goal – we need to make the post-modern system of mutual interdependence and interference universal. Even if we never get there at least this means we know the direction.

We (I am thinking primary of Europe) must start by ensuring that interstate aggression is not permitted. This may mean acting with the USA, our natural allies, to preserve balance when that's the best way preventing aggression. We also need to be ready, on occasion, to restrain the US itself.

We will be able to do this only if the European Union is capable and effective. In fact if there is to be any hope at all of constructing a world in which multilateralism works, our first concern must be to demonstrate success in Europe – something we were doing well until recently. If the EU is seen to be a success, ASEAN, Mercosur and the African Union will follow. For us, this should involve looking again at the parts of the European project that do not work (and there are many of them). It should involve being ready to change and to experiment. It should also involve strengthening cooperation in neglected areas like arms procurement – a single European rifle not a single European army. This would be the single biggest contribution we can make to our security and that of others. There is much else that we need to repair: those of the institutions that are faulty, for example – meaning most of them.

In the end, this short commentary, like the original essay, turns out to be about the European Union. World order begins at home. We have to put our own European house in order if we want to set an example in the world and to influence its future.

Notes

1 Recalling the remark of Karl Kraus: 'How did the war start? Politicians lied to journalists, and then believed what they read in the press.'

7 Why post-liberalism is a dead end in British politics

Britain is too individualistic to turn the clock back

John Gray

While in the halls of academe the suggestion that we live in an era 'after liberalism' is a familiar refrain, it is only in the last few years that dissatisfaction with liberalism has had any resonance in mainstream British politics. The emergence of Blue Labour and Red Toryism has been seen as a symptom of a need to 'go beyond' the liberal values that have shaped the British political consensus over the past couple of decades. It has even been suggested that these movements reflect an emerging post-liberal majority. Against these claims, I suggest that post-liberalism is an incoherent body of ideas, which invokes a historically parochial view of liberalism and denies or rejects some fundamental facts of contemporary British life.

To begin with it is far from clear what post-liberalism actually means. The neo-liberal thinking that influenced the Right from the Eighties onwards articulated only one variety of liberalism – the nineteenth century kind typified by Herbert Spencer, which Hayek revived for a time. Some of the internal contradictions of this type of liberalism, along with the built-in obsolescence of the political project it supported, were explored in my Demos pamphlet *After Social Democracy*, published in 1996, where I harked back to the early twentieth century New Liberalism of J.A. Hobson, L.T. Hobhouse and T.H. Green, who were explicit in rejecting a narrowly individualist understanding of freedom. Even in the nineteenth century, market individualism wasn't the only kind of liberal thinking, or always the most influential. John Stuart Mill had a strong appreciation of the need for enduring social bonds. Keynes was certainly a liberal of some description – just not of the kind that has been in the driving seat during the past few decades. The market-based liberalism which with we are now all too familiar is only a recent version of one strand in a much larger and longer liberal tradition.

Are those who advocate post-liberalism arguing that there are contexts in which liberal values should not apply? Or are they arguing – more plausibly – that liberal values have been too narrowly interpreted as having to do only with personal choice? Some who are now talking about post-liberalism are doing no more than return to a more humanly credible type of liberal thinking. This seems to me to be the case with David Goodhart's critique of recent immigration policy. Is he suggesting there are human needs – for social solidarity and cohesion – that liberalism is unable to acknowledge? That is true only on a view of liberalism that is confined to the recent past. Or is it that the core values of a liberal society are not best served by policies that impose large and rapid changes on large numbers of people? This seems to me to be a more plausible interpretation of Goodhart's argument. But in that case there is nothing 'post-liberal' in suggesting that large-scale immigration might be socially disruptive. One could object that the argument is one-sided: what would Britain have been like *without* mass immigration? A claustrophobic post-imperial redoubt would have been the likely alternative. But if immigration on the scale this country has experienced has come with problems as well as benefits, liberals can recognise the fact without ceasing to be liberal.

The ambiguities of post-liberalism are reflected in the history of the term. When twenty years ago I published *Post-liberalism: studies in political thought*, I intended post-liberalism to mean the view that the liberal way of life was only one form in which the human good can be realised. This wasn't a defence of moral relativism, since I also argued that some values are universally human. Nor was it the claim that liberal societies should retreat from their values. As I put it in the closing lines of the book:

Though it may be only one of the diverse forms of human flourishing our species has achieved, a liberal civil society is the form of society in which we have made our contribution to the human good; and, in defending it, we defend the best in our cultural inheritance, and the best that the species can reasonably hope for.[1]

A very different kind of post-liberalism can be found on the intellectual fringes of British politics at the present time. It would be silly to talk of post-liberalism as composing anything like a coherent system of ideas. A curdled mix of William Morris and Hilaire Belloc does not add up to a political theory. But Red Toryism and Blue Labour do have commonalities, and they are essentially anti-liberal. These are not projects aiming to make liberal values more secure; they are coded attacks on liberalism itself. Lying behind the wildly hyped rhetoric about 'broken Britain' that emanates from both camps is an indignant rejection of the cultural shifts of the Sixties. Both groups look back to a Fifties Britain that – with its drabness and shortages, gender hierarchies and sexual repression – many people hated at the time.

Whatever their excesses, the social upheavals of the Sixties were not the result of a few metropolitan liberals seizing the reins of power. Changes in social and family relations had been underway at least since the Second World War, when millions of women left domestic service and joined the wider economy. The form of life that resulted has not been imposed on a silent majority. Across a wide variety of issues, the British majority is not post-liberal but liberal. Gay marriage may incite fulminating opposition from shrinking numbers of ageing Conservative activists and rancorous elements in the churches. In society at large this civilising measure is hardly an issue at all.

Red Tories and Blue Labourites deny these social facts because they dislike contemporary Britain. If you believe them, a good day for the post-liberal majority would start at Old Harry's Caff, where a cup of coffee costs more than it would at one of the large chains and tastes worse but is consumed in a reassuringly indigenous atmosphere, and continue with a studious avoidance of supermarkets and neighbourly shopping at Aunt Bess's Corner Store. Working life would be a jolly affair conducted in guild-like cooperatives. The communal idyll would be rounded off with a pint of real ale in the snug of the local pub. It is a ridiculous fantasy of a *volkisch* Britain that hasn't the remotest resemblance to a country with which – despite its many blemishes – most people are tolerably content.

It is true that current versions of liberal thinking are in some ways seriously flawed. The rise of UKIP has as much to do with a revolt of the losers from globalisation as with immigration. Old-fashioned social democracy protected the working population from the worst effects of volatile markets; but social democracy depended on steady economic growth, which doesn't look like returning to advanced societies any time soon. The same difficulties undermine the neo-liberal version of social democracy promoted by Blair and inherited by Cameron and Clegg. There has been much chatter about the Big Society, while post-New Labour talks vaguely of moving on from the past. Even though the global market is in disarray, no political leader is ready to confront the downsides of globalisation. Whatever they may say, all three parties remain stuck in neo-liberal dogmas.

The solution isn't to throw out liberal values. It is one thing to argue – as I have done myself – that some social institutions are best operated outside the market. Projecting market forces into the NHS, for example, has resulted in a succession of disasters. That doesn't mean the British majority yearns to throw off the shackles of commodity-fetishism. If they want a different sort of capitalism, it is one that is more intelligently and competently managed. Any party that rejects these facts will soon cease to be electable.

For the foreseeable future, Britain will be a multi-national state harbouring a multi-cultural society – a highly diverse country that can be held together only by liberal values. The practical task is to make this kind of society work. The task is not helped by dystopian visions of communal bliss that have nothing to do with the way most British people live now and want to live in future.

Notes

1 John Gray, *Post-liberalism: studies in political thought*, London, Routledge, 1993, p 328.

8 Britain™ revisited

National identity and patriotism in 2013

Mark Leonard

To an extent that would have been unthinkable in the mid-1990s, the progressive patriotism advocated in Britain™ has become pervasive. A de-racialised, forward-looking identity has been embraced by all the major parties, embodied in the national institutions and broadcast to the world in Danny Boyle's electrifying Olympic closing ceremony. The debate about national identity has literally been turned on its head in the 16 years since Britain™ came out.

In the mid-1990s, national sentiment seemed to be on the wane and the official story revolved around a traditional idea of the country (famously evoked by John Major) that left many younger and ethnic minority Brits feeling unrepresented. But in 2013 Britain is experiencing a surge of patriotism that envelops most citizens – old and new – in a celebration of the values of tolerance and an irreverent pride in the nation's institutional, scientific and cultural heritage. Today, it is white males over the age of 55 who feel left behind – and their radical wing, UKIP, uses the rhetoric of an embattled minority to defend the rights of the old majority.

But while the stories of Britain™ have had much greater resonance and longevity than I ever thought they would in 1997, their very success seems to be holding the political class back from grappling with the new set of challenges.

The genesis of Britain™

Britain™ had an awkward birth. It was due to be published on 1 September 1997. But the day before its publication date, Princess Diana was killed. As the country united in grief, we debated what to do with the report. We delayed its release for a week out of respect but had no idea whether any one would even notice its arrival. In the event, when it was finally released, it played a role in an anguished nation's soul-searching about its identity – part of a national quest for a forward-looking British story.

It immediately precipitated and got swept up in a wave of excitement about Cool Britannia, which was somewhat bewildering for the 23-year-old researcher who suddenly found himself in the centre of a global media furore. Looking back from the vantage point of 2013, it is a surprise to see how many of the ideas at the time have become conventional wisdom.

The starting point for 'rebranding Britain' was a sense that a nation-sized gulf had opened up between the vitality of British culture in the mid-1990s and the introversion and decline of Britain's national institutions and politics. It was also an argument about globalisation and diplomacy – the fact that a country's identity has an impact on its ability to succeed in the world – whether in politics or as a destination for tourists, investment or talent.

There was a sense of malaise in the mid-90s as John Major lost control of his party and the anguish about Europe went hand-in-hand with a collapse in the prestige of British institutions.

Each of the old stories that had defined Britishness since Victorian times seemed to be losing resonance. The 'workshop of the world' had become a service economy. The 'Mother of all Parliaments' and the Royal Family had become soap operas rather than sources of pride – only 20 per cent trusted the monarchy and 13 per cent the House of Commons in 1996. The nation that once defined itself through its Protestant religion in a sea of Catholicism, now had many many faiths and an absence of conspicuous religion. Even the English language was more likely to be associated with Hollywood films.

In 1995, opinion polls showed that half the country said they wanted to emigrate and several British companies were rebranding to hide their origins – Dixons even called its consumer electronics brand Matsui to sound Japanese!

This gloom at home was reflected in how people around the world saw Britain. Polling showed that the overwhelming perceptions were of the UK as a backward-looking anachronism with bad weather, poor food, arrogant and unfriendly people, ubiquitous dirt, arcane rituals and draughty houses.

But this crisis of national identity didn't marry with the dynamism of Britain's cultural life. Instead of mourning the death of the old narratives, Britain™ argued that we should celebrate the birth of new ones, and celebrate some of deeper stories about the country we lived in. In Britain™ I set out to rediscover some other elements of our history that could project into the future. These were distilled into six new national stories that could be debated at home and embodied in attempts to promote Britain to the world:

- The story of 'Hub UK' that saw Britain as the world's cross-roads
- The creative island with big ideas and a history of quirkiness and innovation
- The idea of Britain as a hybrid nation – always mixing diverse elements together into something new rather than trying to protect the 'diginity of difference'
- Open for business – the nation of shop-keepers, a trader
- The silent revolutionary – rather than being a nation of unchanging tradition – first in and first out of the industrial revolution; first to nationalise and then first to privatise
- And finally, the nation of fair play and national solidarity

Many people attacked these stories as an escape from history. That was not my intention at the time: I had been very influenced by the work of historians such as Linda Colley and Eric Hobsbawm who showed how earlier generations of British leaders had reached into our past to create new myths of national unity and invented traditions.

The government was quick to embrace the ideas in the report (not least since Demos's Director Geoff Mulgan was working in Downing Street), and I was placed on a government taskforce charged with advising the Foreign Secretary on how to project Britain overseas. But there was also an immediate backlash.

Some argued that you cannot reduce the complexity of a living country to a brand – I agree, but you can choose which elements of your history and present to emphasise as you engage with the outside world. Others said that it was ridiculous to focus on ephemeral 'coolness' at the expense of longer lasting values. This was in fact one of my biggest frustrations with the debate when the report came out, a national conversation which focused more on which pop stars were invited to Downing Street receptions than the deeper questions about the national character. This was compounded by the shambles of the Millennium Dome, whose vacuous rendition of the national story did a lot of damage to the idea of rebranding Britain.

Changing identity politics

Britain™ was part of a broader attempt by Demos to encourage the left to reclaim the flag (including Philip Dodd's 1994 *Battle over Britain* and a few years later in 2006 a pamphlet by current director David Goodhart *Progressive Nationalism: Citizenship and the Left*). Orwell said in his 'Notes on Nationalism' that the British intelligentsia are suckers for everyone's patriotism but their own. And nowhere was this more true than on the left.

One of the reasons it has struggled electorally is its ambivalence about national identity. Its embrace of Europe, immigration, multiculturalism and constitutional reform meant that its objectives threatened many of the pillars of traditional British identity. We felt that it was urgent for Labour to define a forward-looking, inclusive version of national identity that enabled rather than hindered Britain's embrace of globalisation.

At the time Britain™ was published, no one could foresee the shocks of 9/11 and 7/7, but the inclusive narratives at its core were part of a wider story about stressing commonality across ethnic lines resisting the idea of a clash of civilisations. The Labour government embraced this challenge with gusto – setting out a new national narrative in speeches, and also embracing the idea of citizenship, and challenging essentialist ideas of multiculturalism with a creed of integration. As Sunder Katwala argues, Britain has got beyond asking whether non-whites belong here and is instead focused on asking how we are going to make the 'new us' work. 'Nobody can doubt,' he argues, 'the public appetite is for a shared future – not the fearful, divided and segregated one.'

I should not over-claim for the influence of one pamphlet, but the rehabilitation of an open national story of which it was one part also had an impact on the modernisation of the Conservative Party. It was, in fact, David Cameron and Boris Johnson who represented the modern, outward-looking, multi-racial, multi-ethnic Britain that worships the NHS as its secular religion that was broadcast to the world in Danny Boyle's Olympic opening ceremony.

The ceremony was a near perfect expression of the six narratives of Britain™. And where the debates about national identity in the 1990s were about finding a home for the young, for immigrants, and ethnic minorities in British identity; today's debates are about including white, English men over the age of 55 who feel excluded from the progressive patriotic identity.

UKIP is just a small part of a broader phenomenon spreading across the developed world that resembles a political backlash against globalisation. In focus groups, UKIP supporters reel off a litany of complaints, both imagined and real, about the cultural and social state of Britain. The winners in the Western world now feel threatened by the very things that were previously seen as opportunities. The cheap products and services that they enjoy consuming are now seen as destroyers of jobs. Easy travel is seen as an immigrant flood waiting to happen. The more that globalisation forces countries to bind together, the more citizens crave their independence.

Britain's image abroad

The paradox is that while some Britons are becoming more ambivalent it, the rest of the world is becoming more enthusiastic about them. The project of rebranding Britain seems to have changed the way the world looks at Britain.

At the time that Britain™ was written, many companies were running away from their Britishness and there was a widespread fear that the Union Jack had been captured by the far-right (Italian neo-fascists had taken to wearing it at football matches). But fifteen years later, many companies from other parts of the world have developed a mock British identity, and the Union Jack is more likely to be worn as a fashion accessory by a Japanese hipster than as a political statement by a skinhead. Polling shows that the way Britain is seen internationally has been transformed over the last two decades. A worldwide survey of attitudes organised by the BBC World Service in May 2013 saw Britain come out as the third most popular country in the world.

A few months earlier, Monocle magazine named the UK as the most powerful nation in the world in terms of cultural influence in its annual Soft Power Survey. 'The traditional view of the United Kingdom – bowler hats and umbrellas, royals and high tea – has become tired and clichéd. From sport to design, music to film the UK of the 21st century is rather different than its previous incarnations,' says the survey. 'The Britain that the country has become was best summed up in the opening ceremony of the Olympic Games.'

The future is another country

The Blair-Cameron era of identity building – embodying the progressive patriotism of Britain™ – may now be drawing to a close. It is even possible that the rebranding project has been too successful. Do we need to move on again? And if so how?

From 1945 to 2008, Britain went through ups and downs in its relationship with itself. But although Britain was in competition with other western countries, the continued relevance of the west was not in question. Since 2008 it is.

The western-dominated G8 has given way to the Chinese-dominated G20. The US banking crisis sent our economy into depression. We have lost control of our borders and can't deport terror suspects. People increasingly feel that globalisation is something being done by others to us – rather than something that we are doing to the world. For the last few years, polls have shown that today's Britain expects their children to have less opportunity than their parents.

To the extent that the political parties are dealing with the question of national identity, it is exceedingly defensive – solving the problems of yesterday rather than setting out a pathway to tomorrow. Ed Miliband's embrace of Blue Labour is mirrored by the Tories' attempt to reassure older voters with tough policies on migration, welfare and Europe. Their main goal seems to be making an emotional connection with the lost tribes who are rejecting the new national consensus: a quest to unite a rebranded Olympic Britain with a UKIP Britain mobilised by an angry minority that thinks it is a majority.

What is lacking is a story that makes sense of the current crisis but offers an optimistic way out of it. That project has to go beyond the defensive acknowledgement of the fears of elderly white majority. It must show how Britain can regain its agency in the world by reinventing its economy and state to deliver growth; by transforming our membership of the EU into a platform for power and prosperity; and by reinventing our democracy for an era of social media. All of this means focusing more on changing Britain's internal discourse rather than its projection to the world outside. This means going beyond rebranding Britain, a project whose success may now be inhibiting the necessary quest to update the national story for a new era.

9 The social entrepreneur

How the third sector benefits from an entrepreneurial spirit

Charles Leadbeater

As oxymorons go the social entrepreneur has not done badly, especially considering its modest beginnings.

In 1996 a group of people came to me with a proposition. 'We are social entrepreneurs,' they told me confidently. 'But we are not quite sure what that means.' They wanted help to sort it out.

Those early pioneers included Adele Blakebrough, then running a methadone clinic called Kaleidoscope for drug addicts in Kingston upon Thames and Andrew Mawson, the inspirational founder of the Bromley-by-Bow Centre, much visited by politicians of all stripes.

What I discovered after spending a few weeks exploring what they and others like them did was that social entrepreneurs were addressing social challenges – like providing education and training for young people excluded from school and health services for people with long term conditions – that were not adequately addressed by any other sector.

Charities animated by helping people in need, also often treated the recipients as needy and could trap them in dependence. Social entrepreneurs in contrast saw the people they worked with as capable: the point was to discover and build up their capacity to help themselves. They wanted not just to serve people in need but to raise their ambitions. Mawson would like to say: 'If you ask young people from around here what they want they will tell you a table tennis table and a disco. But if you take them to the Ritz for tea it opens up their minds to something different.'

Business was rarely interested in the poor people and run-down places that social entrepreneurs worked with.

Yet social entrepreneurs stood out not just by adopting business-like practices but also by benchmarking what they did against the kinds of products and services people aspired to as consumers. Touring the beautifully designed Bromley-by-Bow centre Mawson kept saying: 'Just because it's the voluntary sector does not mean it should be second hand and second best. Why shouldn't poor people have great facilities?'

Finally, though public services were invariably present in these communities, they often came in and out, with their own priorities, operating in silos, with little coordination. Public services were too clumsy and top heavy to really engage with what communities needed, they told me. It was like trying to dance with dinosaurs.

Social entrepreneurs operate in the midst of these three forces. They are often animated by the moral imperatives of charity. But they want to work with people and encourage people to devise solutions themselves, rather than just delivering services to people. They seek to address social challenges not just by providing services but by helping people and communities to become more capable, adaptive and self-reliant.

This approach was entrepreneurial, it seemed to me, because they deployed many of the techniques of entrepreneurs, then a phrase still associated with small business and right-wing politics. They sense unmet needs and mobilise resources – often written off buildings and people – to address these needs in ways that generated value. They seek to meet needs that are not met by charity, business or public services.

They achieved this through what seemed at the time to be a bewildering display of ideological cross-dressing. They were both visionary and yet deeply pragmatic. They did not recognise the stereotypes of the compassionate and caring left and ruthless and individualistic right. They would talk to absolutely anyone who would help them achieve their goals. They were socially promiscuous: they would go to any social event hosted by anyone if there was a chance of raising some money or making a new relationship that would help their cause.

The report I wrote, *The Rise of the Social Entrepreneur*, published by Demos in 1997, was certainly not the first to use the term social entrepreneur. Bill Drayton, the former McKinsey consultant and founder of Ashoka, the social entrepreneurs' network had already been using the term to describe his work. In the US the pioneers included Jed Emerson at the Roberts Foundation in San Francisco and Greg Dees at Duke University. In the UK, Michael Young was about to set up the school for social entrepreneurs. Demos did not invent the term social entrepreneur, but it can legitimately claim to have been the first to introduce it to the mainstream media and policy discussion on this side of the Atlantic.

Looking back, what did we get right in that original report, what did we get wrong and what remains unfinished?

What we got right, mainly, was our timing. Social entrepreneurship had developed in the margins: small organisations and slightly oddball people working in marginal communities. Many big ideas start in margins, with people who are slightly deviant and who do not fit into the mainstream. Demos managed to put a name to an emerging practice, which then took off.

The right idea at the right time can help name and shape a movement, but only if it becomes common property, used in many different settings by many people. That is what has happened to the idea of the social entrepreneur. Scores of universities around the world run courses in social entrepreneurship. Impact investment funds, such as Acumen and Impact Ventures, scour the world looking for opportunities, as do the Big Lottery and foundations in the UK. The Skoll World Forum which started in 2003 with 200 people in a lecture theatre at the Said Business School is now a global event attended by thousands with just a hint of Hollywood about it. All over the world people who are trying to create businesses to meet social needs would describe themselves as social entrepreneurs.

Social entrepreneurship has also benefited from the decline in faith in politics. As young people especially have grown disenchanted with mainstream politics as a route to social change, so they have turned to single-issue campaigns and social entrepreneurship as an alternative. With issues such as the environment, trade and food, for example, a mixture of social movements, campaigning and new business models have opened up new consumer markets.

Social entrepreneurship in this more mainstream guise is only likely to continue to grow in reach and importance. In the developing world, solutions to pressing social challenges in the provision of health, education and water in poor communities often depends on businesses with a social mission. When the state cannot or will not provide these public goods then social entrepreneurs are often the only viable alternative. In the developed world we will need more social business skills in both the public and the private sector.

In the public sector, for example in social care, ageing and health, we will need new models of community-based healthcare, which involve people more creatively in managing their own health. Politicians of all persuasions will need social entrepreneurs to help create more effective solutions to shared challenges and to shake up established approaches.

In the private sector, many more businesses are realising that their long-term profitability and ability to deliver for shareholders depends on them demonstrating they also deliver social value as well. The future of mainstream businesses, which are concerned with the externalities of their profit-seeking activities, will depend on how they manage to be social, and how they create shared value.

So far so good. The original *Rise of the Social Entrepreneur* certainly got a couple of things wrong. The first was that the report accepted, rather uncritically, that social entrepreneurs were heroic, lone individuals. The truth is more complicated. The only really successful social ventures are built on teams not individuals. Entrepreneurship involves the combination of different skills, over time, to resolve the multiple challenges a venture will face. Social entrepreneurs only succeed when they are both charismatic but also team players. This is often a difficult combination to pull off.

Many social entrepreneurs are dynamic, charismatic and a pain in the arse. This is not an accident. There is something about the psychic bargain of being a social entrepreneur that pushes people in this direction: they are ambitious but they will not make money. So, much of the reward they get comes from reputation and esteem. Some as a result can seem to live on stage, telling and retelling the story of their success to adoring audiences.

The second mistake was to pit the lonely, heroic social entrepreneur against the clumsy, clodhopping state, as the enemy of change. The truth, again, is more complicated. There are many more people working in public services, at all levels, from head teachers to council chief executives, who see themselves as civic entrepreneurs. They increasingly adopt many of the methods of social entrepreneurs outside the system: spotting needs and opportunities; and trying to mobilise resources from inside and outside the public sector.

All innovation, especially in public services, involves building alliances of consumers, staff, providers and politicians. The early social entrepreneurs presented themselves as outside and against the system. The reality is that there is no alternative to working with the public system and forming alliances with people inside it. Social entrepreneurs will achieve much of their impact by working with and through the public, private and voluntary sectors, rather than going it alone.

Finally, quite a lot of the agenda set out in the original report remains unfinished. Two challenges in particular stand out. One is scale and growth. A great deal of effort, money and attention has been devoted to how social entrepreneurs get started, the early phases of innovation and creativity. The real value, however, lies further down the track, with the less glamorous, hard slog of development and scaling.

This requires a different set of skills which are decidedly unsexy: planning the application of resources; standardising products and processes. Almost two decades after the social entrepreneur burst onto the scene we are still not much further along in understanding the different strategies for how social enterprises scale. Too few of them have. This is only partly an issue of funding and investment. Even if that were available, the skills and understanding to scale social enterprises successfully are still in short supply.

The second is metrics and measures. A lot of work has been done to create measures of social return on investment and blended value. Yet the truth is that too many social enterprises still sell themselves mainly on anecdotes and stories rather than well-grounded numbers and evidence.

The Rise of the Social Entrepreneur helped to kick off a wave of change. Social entrepreneurship has become a global movement involving hundreds of thousands of people. Andrew Mawson is a member of the House of Lords. Adele Blakebrough is a successful social venture capitalist. But if someone were to ask me to revisit the issue now, it would be to write 'The Scale of the Social Entrepreneur', to understand not just how things get started but how and why they spread and scale. That is the big issue facing the movement that the original report helped to get started.

10 The debate over animals

Revisiting the morality of animal rights

Roger Scruton

When Geoff Mulgan asked me to write about the problems of animal rights, in a pamphlet for Demos that was published as *Animal Rights and Wrongs* in 1998, it was at the height of the debate over hunting with hounds, when it was widely assumed that no case could be made for a sport widely considered to be both cruel, and also unnecessary (which seems to be implied by its very description as a 'sport'). My thought, at the time, was that the arguments had been both one-sided, and framed entirely in terms of the utilitarian theory of ethics championed by Peter Singer – a theory that, as Singer himself acknowledges, justifies infanticide and euthanasia, and which certainly has no claim to be the final truth about moral reasoning. Writing the pamphlet (now a book published by Continuum) inspired me to develop a theory of moral reasoning, and to recognise that the problem of animals arises for us because we live the moral life, and they don't.

I have several times had cause to revisit the argument developed in *Animal Rights and Wrongs*. The issues of fishing, fur farming, and the production of animals for food have all been on the political agenda, and it seems that the default position over the last decades has been to side with the animals against the humans. This was particularly apparent in the successful move to ban fur farming. The ban was justified on the grounds that the rearing of captive animals for a 'luxury' product is an offence against 'public morality', and the intrusion of this phrase into the argument – which became more frequent during the 220 hours that Parliament devoted to the question of fox-hunting – made it all the more apparent to me that the disputes are ultimately philosophical.

It is true that the law must, at some level, respond to genuine moral concerns, and cannot be simply out of line with the ordinary conscience. But what exactly is *public* morality, and who is to define it? What happened to Mill's famous argument in *On Liberty* that the coercion of the criminal law can be justified only in order to prevent us from harming others, and never in order to force our compliance to a moral code? What happened to the Wolfenden Report, disapproving the judgement, in *DPP v. Shaw,* which held that there is a common law offence of transgressing 'public morals'? What happened to the argument for the de-criminalisation of homosexuality, despite widespread moral disapproval? What happened to the sovereignty of the individual, which our law has, over the centuries, striven to define and protect?

And why is it so sinful to breed animals for their outer layers, and not for the stuff inside? The MP (Maria Eagle) who introduced the bill to ban fur farming often wears woollen cardigans and leather shoes. But this, it seems, is an offence only against the *private* morality of those who stick to animal-friendly but environmentally destructive materials like nylon and plastic. Thinking about the fur-farming case you might well conclude that it is right to protect animals from people. But liberal thinkers like Mill have always maintained that people also need to be protected from people, not least from the self-righteous moralists who dislike their way of life. The tradition of liberal thinking that was until recently enshrined in our law was the most successful means ever devised to achieve this. And the idea of the law as a guardian of 'public morality' is self-evidently a retreat from that admirable tradition.

Ultimately, however, the recent disputes over animals have not been about human freedom. They have arisen from the love that we feel for animals, and from special pleading on behalf of favoured species. This can be seen very clearly in the activity of the RSPCA, a society that has increasingly devoted itself to policing the rest of us, and punishing the 'animal abusers'. The society is supported by donations from animal lovers, largely from the lovers of cats and dogs. As a result it devotes a great deal of energy to protecting cats from abuse, but none whatsoever to protecting their victims, of which there are 190 million a year in Britain alone. And this distorted morality, which fills ours countryside with destructive predators, while persecuting the humans who allegedly 'abuse' them, forces us to recognise that towards animals, as towards people, there are right and wrong forms of love.

We can love animals as they are, as we imagine them to be, and as we want them to be. The first kind of love is a benefit to animals, the second a threat to them and the third a disaster. It is a general truth about love that it imposes an obligation to know the thing that is loved, to study its needs and desires, and to make sacrifices on its behalf. This obligation involves a cost, and in the case of animals the cost is great. Most people are not prepared to pay that cost. They are not prepared to share the planet openly and honestly with other species, including the species that cannot relate in any obvious way to humans. And instead of loving animals for what they are they love them as substitute humans – creatures whom they can fit out with a human personality, made to their own requirements. This is the 'Bambi' attitude to other species, which requires two shining eyes, a clean body clothed in fur, and behaviour that can be interpreted, with a small dose of imagination, as expressing quasi-human affections. It is common among cat-lovers, most of whom imagine that cats reciprocate their affection, and most of whom are largely indifferent to the enormous destruction and suffering that they cause. A real animal-lover would regard the domestic cat as a threat, to be controlled in the same way as rats are controlled.

To love animals properly we must first recognise that they are *not* humans, and not capable of human love, which is premised on the freedom of its object. Love between humans involves moral judgement, accountability, respect and a disinterested desire for the other's good. It involves personality and choice. It may begin in need and dependence, but its value consists in the fact that it can grow beyond that point, to become a condition of mutual giving and willing sacrifice. Animals are not capable of this, even if they can show the greatest attachment to their masters, like dogs who die in their master's defence. Making clear the difference here, between intense animal attachment and self-sacrificing love is difficult, and I have taken up the theme in more recent writings.

My argument in *Animal Rights and Wrongs* stemmed, not from a disrespect for animals, but from a respect for moral reasoning, and for the concepts – right, duty, obligation, virtue – which it employs and which depend at every point on the distinctive features of self-consciousness. I argued that animals do not have rights, and are threatened by our beliefs to the contrary. Elevated to the plane of moral consciousness, they find themselves unable to respond to the distinctions that morality requires. They do not distinguish right from wrong; they cannot recognise the call of duty or the binding obligations of the moral law. And because of this we judge them purely in terms of their ability to share our domestic ambience, to profit from our affection, and from time to time to reciprocate it in their own mute and dependent way. And it is precisely this which engenders our unscrupulous favouritism – the favouritism that has made it a crime to shoot a cat, however destructive its behaviour, but a praiseworthy action to poison a mouse, and thereby to infect the food chain on which so many animals depend.

It is not that we should withdraw our love from our favourite animals: to the extent that they depend on that love to that extent we should continue to provide it. But we must recognise that by loving them as *individuals* we threaten the animals who cannot easily be loved in any such way. Loving our dogs and cats we put a strain upon the natural order that is felt most grievously by the birds and beasts of the field. And even if those creatures have no rights, this does not cancel the fact that we have duties towards them – duties that become more serious and demanding every day, as we humans expand to take over the habitats that we confiscate without scruple and enjoy without remorse. And our lack of scruple is only amplified by the sentimental attitudes that are nurtured by the love of pets, and which inculcate in us the desire for easy-going, cost-free and self-congratulatory affections, and which thereby undermine the human virtue on which the rest of nature most depends.

11 Relational justice

The power of networks in rehabilitation

Danny Kruger

In 1998 Demos was based near Blackfriars, in a building on the site of the old Bridewell prison. It was a cheerful place: the team had one foot in Downing Street and, they rightly imagined, years of happy left-liberal policy-making ahead of them. I was the token Tory, working two days a week while studying for a post-grad history degree. To further distance me from the 18th century, Perri 6, the de facto boss while Geoff Mulgan was at No. 10, gave me the task of writing about the internet. I proudly published *Access Denied? Preventing information exclusion*.

Access Denied? has not aged well. Reading it is to travel back to the beginnings of the 'information superhighway' when, indeed, the promise of the internet was the transmission of more information, more quickly – and when 'information' meant data held by sources of authority, which could now be passed to citizens and consumers down a fibre-optic cable. Among other suggestions, my paper proposed 'ICT kiosks' where people 'without personal computers and modems' could 'access services' provided by the state.

15 years on, the volume and speed of information travelling from power to the people seems a minor, almost insignificant feature of the modern age. The critical development has been the opportunity the internet presents for interaction *between* people, within groups which form and reform without reference to established power. The internet is not a bulletin board but a café, albeit with some useful information on the wall; its primary function is to enable socialising, professional networking and the organic development of ideas.

This principle – we might call it relationism – has been a theme of the 21st century. Information, opportunities and skills were the currency of the 20th century. Today we see that your wealth consists in your network, in the 'weak ties' long ago identified by Mark Granovetter as the key to professional success. *Access Denied?* might have heralded an age in which digital communications spread this wealth more fairly, or, conversely, further entrenched the privileges of the networked few. It didn't.

Today I run a charity, Only Connect, which I set up with my wife in 2006. We work with prisoners, ex-offenders and young people at risk of offending. And the experience has confirmed, in a hundred anecdotes, what the research tells us: that relationism is key. The culture and attitudes held by groups are of infinitely greater power to affect behaviour than any criminal law, let alone the customary sermonising by the judge during sentencing.

Yet public policy, especially in criminal justice, remains uncomfortable with this reality. Take its most concrete expression. New prisons today are still built on the design of the Victorian reformers who – appalled at the messy squalor of places like Bridewell – created hygienic temples to personal reform: batteries of individual cells connected only by narrow walkways, with opportunities for socialising (except in the chapel) deliberately designed out.

They are built like that today because it is cheaper to manage large populations when they're banged up 20 hours a day, with a single officer keeping an eye on a landing which houses 100 men. But they also reflect a mindset about justice that remains prevalent throughout the system.

Rightly, criminal justice is seen as a matter between the individual and the state. The defendant is denuded of all relations, standing alone in the dock; he faces, in the legal apparatus, the anonymous incarnation of society – blind justice, concerned only with the facts of guilt or innocence.

So it should be, for we are free agents, carrying personal responsibility and rightfully liable for the consequences of our wrongdoing. As CS Lewis said, said the only proper basis of punishment is 'desert'; any other reason for inflicting hardship on someone – e.g. for 'deterrence' or 'cure' – is tyranny. There has been a sad falling-off in this classical liberal principle. Those who disdain retribution deny criminals their most basic human right of all, the right to be regarded and treated as an independent moral actor. The recognition of this right is the beginning of personal reformation.

But that is only the foundation, and the least interesting part of the building. On top we need to build the sort of home humans can live in. Because if we have forgotten the basis of punishment we have also lost sight of how to rehabilitate.

Justice is a transaction between the individual offender and society as a whole, incarnated in the state. But crime is not. A hundred tributaries lead to the main current of criminal motivation: a network of social interactions makes the moral atmosphere in which the individual operates. Similarly, at the other end, there is the opportunity to increase an offender's chance of going straight if we make him part of a network which preaches and practices different norms. An offender's relationships get him into crime; they – or different ones – are what will get him out of it.

What might a relational justice policy look like? For a start, it should enable us to open prisons up to the communities they serve. Security has become a fetish for prisons, with a sense of hostile suspicion of all visitors, volunteers or 'civilian' (i.e. not Prison Service) staff. The only relationships many prisoners are able to form are with prison officers who, as a general group, are not frequently optimistic about the idea of rehabilitation.

Prisons can and should be community institutions, rooted in the neighbourhood whence criminals come and whither they will return, open to all the practical support and positive moral influences the community can provide. Instead of Victorian barracks, we need prisons that enable pro-social norms to develop – like the modern therapeutic communities which have been so successful with sex offenders.

Further, as the above analysis suggests, we might look at separating the punishment purpose from the rehabilitative purpose. 'Two-stage sentencing' would mean that offenders are handed, first, their punishment – a duration of imprisonment appropriate to the awfulness of their crime, without reference to their needs or circumstances or likelihood of re-offending; and second, their rehabilitation package, which is constructed around their personal strengths and needs and is designed to help them go straight.

An otherwise law-abiding, mentally well woman who killed her husband during a row would face a long punishment phase, fitting to the seriousness of the crime, followed by a short rehabilitation phase to reintegrate her into normal life. A prolific shoplifter with a chronic heroin addiction might require 6 weeks behind bars for his latest offence, followed by 12 months on strict conditions in a residential rehabilitation centre. In both cases the key consideration during the rehabilitation phase is the social network the offender will be part of.

I malign the 20th century (and every century before) by suggesting that 'relationism' is the idea of the 21st. Not only were thinkers of left and right, like Amitai Etzioni and David Willetts, already talking in these terms while I sat in Bridewell Place in 1998 thinking up individualistic responses to the digital revolution; the ideas of connectedness, relationship and belonging as the goal of social policy is as old as Aristotle. What we call post-liberalism is re-heated pre-liberalism.

But there is nevertheless an opportunity now for a return to these truths. As globalisation is unhooking people from their traditional allegiances, the yearning for community grows stronger. And of course the engine of globalisation, digital technology, can help. What people at risk of offending need is social networks which are pro-social not anti-social. And perhaps we can build online systems which, both in and outside prison, shape the individual's community to support their rehabilitation.

12 The good life

Wellbeing at a time of declining incomes

Amitai Etzioni

If the people of the world cannot return to what is being called the old normal (paid for by strongly growing economies), what will the new normal look like? Will it simply be a frustrating and alienating scaled-back version of the old normal? Or will the people develop new concepts of what a good life made, as they did in earlier historical periods? If successful, a recharacterisation of the good life will allow people to turn their misery into an opportunity.

The good life in an historical and transnational perspective

People immersed in the consumerist culture that prevails now in large parts of the world's civilisations find it difficult to imagine a good life that is based on rather different values to those they live by. However, throughout history, different conceptions of what makes a good life have arisen. For instance, for centuries the literati of imperial China came to prominence not through acquisition of wealth, but through pursuit of knowledge and cultivation of the arts. They spent years memorising the Confucian classics.

Sociologist Reinhard Bendix writes that in keeping with Confucian teachings:

The educated man must stay away from the pursuit of wealth... because acquisitiveness is a source of social and personal unrest. To be sure, this would not be the case if the success of economic pursuits was guaranteed, but in the absence of such a guarantee the poise and harmony of the soul are jeopardized by the risks involved... The cultured man strives for the perfection of the self, whereas all occupations that involve the pursuit of riches require a one-sided specialization that acts against the universality of the gentleman.[1]

During the Middle Ages, knights were expected to adhere to an exacting code of chivalry. In traditional Jewish communities, studying the Torah was considered the preferred way of life.

Even in recent Western history, there were significant changes in what was viewed as the good life. Economists noted that during WWII, the American productive capacity greatly expanded. They feared that with the end of the war, the idling of the assembly lines that produced thousands of tanks, planes, and many war-related materials would lead to massive unemployment – because there was nothing that the assembly lines could produce that people needed, given that their fixed needs were sated.

In the years that followed WWII, industrial corporations discovered that they could produce needs for the products they were marketing. For instance, first women and then men were taught that they smelled poor and needed to purchase deodorants. Men, who used to wear white shirts and grey flannel suits like a uniform, learned that they 'had to' purchase a variety of shirts and suits, and that last year's wear was not proper in the year that followed. The same was done for cars, ties, handbags, towels and sheets, sunglasses, watches and numerous other products. Vance Packard lays this all out in his best-selling book, *The Hidden Persuaders.*

In later decades, as more and more women joined the labour force, the incomes from husband and wife combined went to paying for the high-consumption lifestyle. More and more people began to take their work home with them, even on holidays, courtesy of BlackBerry smart phones and their equivalents.

In short, there is nothing natural or unavoidable about what is considered the affluent life; It entails the kind of lifestyle that was considered worthy of contempt by previous societies and in early historical periods of the West.

Laying the foundation for a new society

Today, one finds millions of people who already have moved in the direction of less-is-more, although they are hardly yet following a vision of a new good society or coming together to promote it. These millions include a large number of senior citizens who retired before they had to, to allow more time for alternative pursuits.

These seniors typically lead what might be called a comfortable life from a materialistic viewpoint, but spend more of their time socialising and engaged in politically active, spiritual, and cultural pursuits, rather than continuing to be employed and consume full throttle. The same holds for the millions of women who decide not to return to work after they have children, at least until they reach school age, and many for much longer, although this means that they will have to consume less.

As these two large groups, as well as those who drop out of high-earning pursuits to follow a more 'meaningful' life – say, as teachers for those less privileged – illustrate, one need not lead a life of sackcloth and ashes, of deprivation and sacrifice. One can work enough to ensure one's basic creature comforts but dedicate the rest of one's resources, energy, and aspirations to goods other than consuming more, and one can find more satisfaction in alternative pursuits to working long and hard to pay for consumption above and beyond what is needed for a comfortable life.

The main alternatives

Consumerism has long been shown to not provide contentment (or happiness). The data, as most social science data, are complex. Not all the correlations yield the same results.[2] However, overviews of the data have repeatedly concluded that after income rises above a given level, additional income buys little happiness. Japan is an often-cited example. Between 1962 and 1987, Japan's economy more than tripled its GNP per capita. Yet Japan's overall happiness remained constant over that period.[3] In 1970, Americans' average income could buy over 60 per cent more than it could in the 1940s, yet the average happiness had not increased[4].

At high income and consumption levels, additional consumption (and the work required to afford it) lead people to deny themselves alternative pursuits. It seems a form of fixation. It has been referred to as a hedonic treadmill.

These data ought now to be re-examined, as many middle and working class people face not so much giving up additional income (and obsessive consumption) in order to free time and resources for alternative pursuits – but are forced to give up the dream of an affluent life based on high and rising levels of consumption. Can they come to see such capping not as a source of frustration but as an opportunity to reexamine their priorities? The analogue is to a worker who finds that he is furloughed one day each week and hence works only four days, but finds that the extra day offers a welcome opportunity to spend more time with the kids or going fishing – not to someone who lost his job.

The alternatives

The main alternative pursuits that generate much more contentment than consumerism are very familiar and hence visited next very briefly.

Social activities

Individuals who spend more time with their families, friends, in social clubs, and in communal activities – those who do not bowl alone – are more content than those less socially active. An analysis of nearly 150 studies found that individuals with stronger social relationships exhibited a 50 per cent increased likelihood of survival.[5] Robert E. Lane writes, 'Most studies agree that a satisfying family life is the most important contributor to well-being... The joys of friendship often rank second.'[6] Robert Putnam presents a mountain of data to the same effect.

Spiritual and religious activities

Individuals who spend more time living up to the commands of their religion (attending church, praying, fasting, making pilgrimages and doing charity work), studying for studying's sake rather than as a vocation, or engaged in cultural activities such as painting or making music, not to serve a market but for the intrinsic enjoyment, are more content than those less so engaged. For example, studies have demonstrated that people with a deep religious faith are healthier, live longer, and have lower rates of divorce, crime, and suicide.[7] To cite but one study, Robert Putnam and David Campbell found that the difference in happiness between an American who goes to church once a week and someone who does not attend church was 'slightly larger than the difference between someone who earns $10,000 a year and his demographic twin who earns $100,000 a year.'[8]

Community involvement

Researchers who examined the effect of community involvement found a strong correlation with happiness. One study, which evaluated survey data from 49 countries, found that membership in (non-church) organisations has a significant positive correlation with happiness.[9] Derek Bok notes, 'Some researchers have found that merely attending monthly club meetings or volunteering once a month is associated with a change in wellbeing equivalent to a doubling of income.'[10] Other studies have found that individuals who devote substantial amounts of time to volunteer work have greater life satisfaction.[11]

Two bonuses

A society in which capping consumption is the norm and majorities find much of their contentment in transcendental pursuits will gain two bonuses of much import. One is obvious and one much less so.

Obviously, a good life that combines a cap on consumption and work with dedication to transcendental pursuits is much less taxing on the environment than consumerism and the level of work that paying for it requires. This is the case because transcendental activities require relatively few scarce resources, fossil fuels, or other sources of physical energy. Social activities (such as spending more time with one's children) require time and personal energy but not large material or financial outlays.

For example, often those who spend large amounts of money on their kids' toys or entertainment bond less with them than those whose relations are much less mediated by objects.

The same holds for cultural and spiritual activities such as prayer, meditation, enjoying and making music, art, sports, and adult education. True, consumerism has turned many of these pursuits into expensive endeavors. However, one can break out of this mentality and find that it is possible to engage in most transcendental activities quite profoundly using a moderate amount of goods and services. One does not need designer clothes to enjoy the sunset or shoes with fancy labels to benefit from a hike. Chess played with plastic pieces is the same game as the one played with carved mahogany or marble pieces. And the Lord does not listen better to prayers read from a leather-bound Bible than those read from a plain one, printed on recycled paper. In short, the transcendental society is much more sustainable than consumeristic capitalism.

Much less obvious are the ways the transcendental society serves social justice. Social justice entails transferring wealth from those disproportionally endowed to those who are underprivileged. A major reason such reallocation of wealth has been surprisingly limited in free societies is that those who command the 'extra' assets tend also to be those who are politically powerful. Promoting social justice by organising those with less and forcing those in power to yield has had limited success in democratic countries and led to massive bloodshed in others. Hence the quest for other ways to reduce the resistance of the elites to the reallocation of wealth.

There are many ways of living a good life. Reshaping it in the ways that I have suggested will not only spare the world major social and political upheavals and international conflicts but also make it into world in which all the people can flourish.

Notes

1 Reinhard Bendix, 'Max Weber: an intellectual portrait,' p 124.

2 See Ruut Veenhoven and Michael Hagerty, 'Rising Happiness in Nations 1946 – 2004,' *Social Indicators Research*. 79: 3: 421 – 436; Betsey Stevenson and Justin Wolfers, 'Economic Growth and Subjective Well-Being: Reassessing the Easterlin Paradox,' *Brookings Papers on Economic Activity*, Spring 2008, 69: p 1 – 87.

3 Richard Easterlin, 'Diminishing Marginal Utility of Income? Caveat Emptor,' *Social Indicators Research,* 2005.

4 Richard Easterlin, 'Does Money Buy Happiness,' *The Public Interest*, 30 (Winter 1973).

5 Julianne Holt-Lunstad, Timothy B. Smith, and J. Bradley Layton, 'Social Relationships and Mortality Risk: A Meta-analytic Review,' *PLoS Medicine*, 7:7 (July 2010).

6 Robert E. Lane, 'Does Money Buy Happiness?' *Public Interest*, Fall 1993, p 58.

7 Derek Bok, *The Politics of Happiness: What Government Can Learn from the New Research on Well Being,* Princeton, NJ: Princeton University Press, 2010, p 21 – 22.

8 Robert D. Putnam and David E. Campbell, *American Grace: How Religion Divides and Unites Us,* New York, Simon and Schuster, 2010, p 491.

9 John F. Helliwell, 'Well-Being, Social Capital and Public Policy: What's New?' *Economic Modelling*, 20:2, March 2003, p 331 – 360.

10 Bok, p 20.

11 Bok, p 22.

13 Valuing culture

Assessing the contribution of Britain's cultural institutions

John Holden

In June 2003 Demos organised a conference called 'Valuing Culture'[1] to debate the relationship between government and the cultural sector. Since the turn of the millennium, senior figures from the arts world had been complaining that government had lost sight of why it should fund culture, and now the voices were getting louder. Many felt that the balance had tipped away from supporting culture as a public good in its own right, and instead government was only interested in funding the arts and heritage in order to achieve economic and social goals.

I had personal experience of this. The target-driven obsessions of Downing Street had filtered down to local level, and the music venue of which I was Chairman had been offered a grant – subject to the condition that it would be used to promote road safety for schoolchildren. We toyed with the idea of forcing a connection between Saint-Saëns' Carnival of the Animals and Zebra crossings, but eventually turned the money down until it was offered on a more sensible basis.

The disconnection between political and artistic priorities was clear, but understandable. Politicians want to pursue economic and social goals for their community or their country – that is, after all, their job – but artists and audiences are more interested in their individual experiences. Members of the public do not sit in a darkened auditorium thinking 'I'm so glad this theatre is contributing to regional regeneration and tourism targets.' People want laughter, thrills, tears and torment from their art. Government had lost sight of this.

The then Secretary of State for Culture, Tessa Jowell, who spoke at the conference, agreed that there was a problem, and soon afterwards she wrote a personal essay, *Government and the*

Value of Culture, in which she asked: 'how, in going beyond targets, can we best capture the value of culture?'

I thought this an interesting and pressing question. Politicians and cultural practitioners needed to find some shared terms of engagement that would foster a healthy relationship between them. In turn, a well-functioning cultural 'system' would ultimately benefit all of us: artists would find an audience, children would get a cultural education, cultural organisations would flourish, and the politicians would, paradoxically, get what they wanted when the art itself was freed from the tyranny of targets.

So I decided to try to tackle Tessa Jowell's question myself. Although the subject was widely recognised as being important, it proved impossible to get any funding to investigate it (a common experience for think-tankers), but some of the initial thinking appeared in a report that Robert Hewison and I were commissioned to write as a result of the conference: *Challenge and Change, HLF and Cultural Value* (2004), which helped to shape the Heritage Lottery Fund's next strategic plan. As a result of writing in the evenings and at weekends, what eventually emerged over the next six years was a series of Demos pamphlets, some co-authored with Robert Hewison and Sam Jones.

The main pamphlets were titled *Capturing Cultural Value: How culture has become a tool of government policy; Cultural Value and the Crisis of Legitimacy: Why Culture needs a Democratic Mandate;* and *Democratic Culture: Opening up the Arts to Everyone.* Reading them in sequence shows a developing idea, as I increasingly realised that the enquiry was not limited to describing 'cultural value', but also involved exploring the relationships between various parts of the cultural system, and seeing how differing concerns about value affected different people.

The articulation of cultural value always sits within specific historical circumstances. For the past twenty years 'the value of culture' has been debated in the context of a fractious relationship between on the one hand cultural practitioners, who are exasperated at having to repeat, over and again, the many and varied arguments that justify their public funding, and on the other successive political office-holders, each of whom needs to discover why film makers and theatre directors don't, and can't, back only 'winners'.

As I saw it, my task was to try to make sense of culture by developing a framework that could accommodate many different methods of valuing culture (artistic, aesthetic, economic and social), and different perspectives (those of cultural professionals, politicians, and members of the – very diverse – public). I was attempting to create understanding in the space between abstract philosophical enquiry about the nature of 'culture' and 'the arts', and the minutiae of evaluating particular cultural forms, organisations or events. Academia was concerned with ideas, and cultural consultants were busy looking at specific practice, but there was a gap in the middle. I wanted to solve the practical problem that local authority arts officers faced when putting the case for culture to their Councillors. People working in the arts, heritage or libraries needed to be able to articulate, in straightforward terms, why they were important to society.

The framework that evolved identified three ways of looking at value: intrinsic, instrumental, and institutional value. 'Intrinsic' means 'essential to' or 'integral to', so intrinsic value implies that distinct forms of culture – dance, theatre, literature and so on – have a value in their own right. You cannot sing a dance or build a poem; each art form provides unique means of expression, and if any of them were destroyed humanity would be impoverished. It seems to me therefore that governments have a duty to maintain the health of art forms for current and future generations because they are public goods that cannot be replicated in other ways.

But 'intrinsic value' has also been used to express two other aspects of culture. First, the term acts as shorthand for the way in which art forms have individual, subjective effects on each of us. Here we are dealing in hard-to-measure abstract and intangible concepts like beauty, pleasure, revulsion, and the sublime. Second, intrinsic value is used as a proxy for 'artistic excellence', and the defence of 'intrinsic values' has become a rallying point for people who believe in 'art for art's sake' – sometimes in order to maintain the status of a cadre of experts who make judgments about quality on behalf of the rest of us.

For them, the second type of value, instrumental value, is anathema. 'Instrumental value' involves the use of culture as a tool or instrument to accomplish some other aim – such as economic regeneration, or improved exam results, or better patient recovery times. The problems with measuring the instrumental effects of culture are legion,[2] but there can be no doubt that they exist. Indeed, some cultural organisations have instrumental values at the heart of their practice, such as trying to rehabilitate prisoners or help the homeless through what they do.

Intrinsic and instrumental values describe what happens in a cultural encounter in two different ways, but on their own they do not adequately allow for an investigation of the important role that cultural organisations play in the cultural system. This is why, in *Cultural Value and the Crisis of Legitimacy,* and influenced by Mark Moore's book *Creating Public Value,*[3] I suggested a third type of value – institutional value – which was later explored in depth in another Demos pamphlet, *Not a Sideshow,* by Robert Hewison.

Institutional value refers to the social goods created (or destroyed) by cultural organisations. Such organisations are part of the public realm, and *how* they do things creates value as much as *what* they do. In their interactions with the public, cultural organisations are in a position to increase – or indeed decrease – such things as our trust in each other, our idea of whether we live in a fair and equitable society, our mutual conviviality and civility, and a whole host of other public goods. Institutional value should therefore be counted as part of the contribution of culture to producing a democratic and well-functioning society, and is another reason why culture should be funded by the state.

Bringing institutional value into the debate also had the advantage of undermining the fruitless polarity associated with intrinsic and instrumental values.

The process of triangulation allowed for a multi-disciplinary approach, because intrinsic, instrumental and institutional values could each be explored in depth using different intellectual disciplines, deploying different techniques of measurement and assessment.

The three values types are viewpoints or perspectives of equal validity, and they must be considered together. For example, if a schoolchild is taken on a school visit to a museum, she may well have a moving emotional experience that can be talked about using the language of intrinsic value; she may be taught about an artist, and reproduce her learning in the exam room, and that becomes a measurable instrumental benefit. And she may get a sense of civic pride from this local museum, feel part of her community, and see the museum as a public place that she is entitled to share with others – and that would be an example of institutional value. Similarly, each cultural organisation will strike a different balance in its own pursuit of cultural value: one might emphasise artistic experimentation, another their educational role and a third their service to the local community.

In 2013, the cultural value question is still alive: the Arts and Humanities Research Council has recently launched a major £2m project to 'advance our understanding of the value of culture.' This is needed because the gap between the nuance of describing the multi-faceted value of culture and the crude reductionism of the Treasury Green Book has not yet been bridged.

Recent proof of this occurred in April this year, when the current Secretary of State for Culture, Maria Miller, gave a woeful speech in which she reportedly told an audience of cultural grandees that 'the arts world must make the case for public funding by focusing on its economic, not artistic, value.'[4] This must have provoked intense exasperation on the part of her audience, most of whom would remember the 1988 publication of John Myerscough's *The Economic Importance of the Arts,*[5] and the dozens of economic impact reports in the years since; not to mention John Tusa's observation in 1999 that 'Mozart is Mozart because of his music and not because he created a tourist industry in Salzburg.'[6]

The cultural world is regularly asked to provide 'evidence', but the idea that policy in the rest of government always rests on hard evidence is nonsense. Education policy is made on the basis of quixotic beliefs and hunches as much as on evidence. HS2 provides a further example: when government figures for economic benefit were called into question by the National Audit Office, the Transport Secretary defaulted to an emotional argument: 'We are not building HS2 simply because the computer says 'yes'. We are building it because it is the right thing to do to make Britain a stronger and more prosperous place.'[7]

The Demos pamphlets did not settle the question of cultural value, but I think they did influence the relationship between some cultural organisations and the public. In *Cultural Value and the Crisis of Legitimacy*, I argued that the cultural world was spending too much time and energy on discussions with funders when it should be concentrating on improving its interactions with the public, who ultimately controlled the funders through the ballot box, and who were the intended beneficiaries of funding.

I saw culture then, and see it now, not as something that is delivered by cultural organisations to the public, but as something created through the interaction between them. The more sophisticated the dialogue between citizens and cultural organizations, the better it would be for both of them.

In this area there has been some progress. In 2006 Arts Council England launched a 'Public Value inquiry' in an attempt to find out the public's views about the arts, and the Heritage Lottery Fund held focus groups to find out what people thought 'heritage' meant. Following the publication of the pamphlets, arts organisations all over the world have been in touch to find out more.

So what next? I think politicians of all stripes still fail to understand the importance of the arts and culture. Since Demos' cultural value work began in 2003, culture has become more central to many policy areas, from the economy, where a recent report from NESTA estimates that in 2010 the creative economy accounted for 9.7 per cent of UK GVA,[8] to foreign relations, to the politics of identity. New technology has transformed communication, and the content of much of that communication is cultural. Nowadays we are what we read, listen to, watch and create.

But Whitehall and Westminster still think of culture as leisure and recreation, and confine it to the smallest government department. Culture should be a central concern of the Department for Education, the Treasury, the Home Office and the Foreign Office. All Departments should have a Chief Cultural Adviser, just as they all (except DCMS) have a Chief Scientific Adviser, but the prospect of that happening seems very distant. If government understood the full range of value that culture generates, rather than concentrating only on its economic impact, they would stand a better chance of doing a good job for their citizens.

Notes

1 The conference was jointly organised with AEA Consulting, hosted by the National Gallery and the National Theatre, and funded by the Clore Duffield Foundation and the Jerwood Foundation

2 See Selwood S, 'The Politics of Data Collection: Gathering analysing and using data about the subsidised cultural sector in England', in *Cultural Trends*, Volume 12, Issue 47, 2002.

3 Moore M, *Creating Public Value: Strategic Management in Government,* Harvard University Press, Cambridge, MA, 1995.

4 'Maria Miller: Arts must make economic case', BBC News, available at www.bbc.co.uk/news/entertainment-arts-22267625 (accessed 15 July 2013).

5 Myerscough J, *The Economic Importance of the Arts in Britain,* London: Policy Studies Institute, 1988.

6 Tusa J, *Art Matters: Reflecting on Culture,* Methuen, London, 1998.

7 'High Speed Rail 2 business case ridiculed by National Audit Office', Telegraph, available at www.telegraph.co.uk/news/uknews/road-and-rail-transport/10060087/High-Speed-Rail-2-business-case-ridiculed-by-National-Audit-Office.html (accessed 15 July 2013).

8 Bakhshi H et al, *A Manifesto for the Creative Economy,* Nesta, London, 2013, p 33.

14 A brief history of personalisation

How a user focus has rolled back paternalistic cultures of public service

Claudia Wood

Personalisation has been game changing for public services in the UK, and has fundamentally changed the relationship between citizens and the state. Over the past decade, top-down, paternalistic cultures of public service have ceded to consumer choice, empowerment and the idea of service users being 'experts by experience'. Such concepts – all under the banner of personalisation – are now so entrenched in public service design that it would be unthinkable to turn back. Demos – an organisation founded on the principle that policy research should be 'of the people' and capture the voice of those affected by those policies – took personalisation to its heart early on. We have played a part in challenging the thinking around personalisation ever since.

In the early 2000s, key Demos thinkers – Charlie Leadbeater, Tom Bentley, Sophia Parker and others – were already testing the boundaries of personalisation, seeing its most common interpretation at that time (choice between public services) as a shallow driver of public service reform. In Demos's influential *Personalisation through Participation*, Charlie Leadbeater explored a range of more radical applications of personalisation beyond consumer-led theories of change. He outlined five distinct interpretations of personalisation: a better customer interface (i.e. improvements in using traditional services), help in navigating such services (e.g. through advice or advocacy), being in control of one's funding allocation (such as personal budgets), co-production between service user and provider, and finally, the self-organisation of service users to develop new services independent from the state.

The fifth interpretation, Charlie reasoned, would be the most revolutionary – where individuals would be able to come together to create innovative new solutions to intractable problems. It went beyond incremental reform within traditional services to the bottom-up creation of entirely new models and, in turn, implied an entirely new role for the state: no longer providing or commissioning services, but creating forums for community groups to come together and design their own services.

But it was many years before this radical notion was revisited as a credible form of personalisation, in part due to the ascendance of personal budgets – one tool through which personalisation could be achieved – which left many of the alternatives overlooked for several years.

Personal budgets came about through a marriage of person-centred thinking and direct payments (the financial transfer of social care funding from the local authority to the individual to purchase their own care), and captured the imagination of policy makers and practitioners alike as a particularly promising means of giving users both choice between and a sense of control over services. In 2007 the government signalled its commitment to personal budgets with the launch of the Ministerial Concordat *Putting People First*, establishing a collaboration between local and national government, the care sector and regulator to work towards shared aims to transform adult social care, with personalisation as a central theme. £520 million was given to local authorities over the three years from 2008 to facilitate this.

Demos once again explored the innovative potential of personal budgets, with the 2008 *Making it Personal* declaring them to be:

The most effective way of personalising public services – when self-directed services are introduced with the right kind of support for people and their choices translate into how money is spent they deliver huge pay-offs...

Between 2008 and 2010, Demos worked with several local authorities to survey the local population using social care, in order to find out what they might spend their personal budgets on. These insights helped many local authorities prepare for the shift to personal budgets and look hard at their local facilities on offer. The findings, published in *At Your Service I* and *II* and *Personal Best*, pointed to a significant impact on care services, as people were likely to move from traditional models of day centre and home care to more pioneering forms of support, such as personal assistants, and support for employment, volunteering, social and sporting activities.

But it soon became clear that the original interpretation of personal budgets – financial control married with self-directed support and as a tool for participation – was being narrowed, while at the same time other forms of personalisation were being crowded out. In 2009 targets were set, stating that all new recipients of state funded care should be offered a personal budget by 2010, and by 2011 30 per cent of state funded care users should be using a personal budget.

In 2010, under the new government, personal budget take-up was deemed 'disgraceful' and a new, more challenging target was set – 100 per cent take-up of personal budgets by 2013.

What had been envisaged by Demos and others as a form of empowerment within an arsenal of personalisation tools was becoming a financial mechanism, whereby care users were tasked with commissioning their own care (often with less money than before). Not only had the evolution of personalisation stalled at number three in Charlie's list of five, but the pressures of austerity was seeing it turn into something far less revolutionary than what was intended.

Demos took this on in our 2011 report *Tailor Made*, which criticised the excessive focus on personal budget take-up as a proxy for personalisation and suggesting targets be dropped or adjusted to recapture the wider understanding of personalisation first developed in our earlier reports. This work once again explored different methods of personalisation, brought up to date to face the social and economic challenges of austerity. It included coproduction, democratic engagement, and – as Leadbeater first envisioned – self organised peer-support as a form of service delivery. The conclusion was that the way in which personalisation was achieved should in itself be personalised, making it achievable for all groups, even if they weren't able or willing to handle a personal budget.

We were not alone in our critique – the Association of Directors of Adult Social Services (ADASS) subsequently called for the overhaul of the social care personal budget target in 2012 – and later that year Norman Lamb, Minister for Care, announced the 100 per cent target would be replaced by a more realistic 70 per cent. But is this not simply a more forgiving variation on the same targets-driven theme?

Fortunately, the Coalition Government's interest in devolution and Big Society-style solutions created a space to think more creatively about local approaches to personalised services, and in 2010, *Putting People First* was replaced with *Think Local Act Personal* (TLAP). This new programme, led by a broad coalition of organisations, is dedicated to delivering personalisation from the bottom up. This has led to a more varied and richer understanding of personalisation, with *Making it Real* launched in 2012. This is a set of indicators developed by disabled people and their families to mark progress towards personalisation, including using co-production and providing information and advice to ensure people are more involved in decisions about their care.

While we are in a very positive place now, over the last 10 years, personalisation has seen ebbs and flows – from choice to self-directed support, to a narrower financial take on personal budgets, to co-production and participation once more. It has been influenced by prevailing political moods and, latterly, economic realities. But there is no doubt it has permanently reshaped people's expectations of public services.

As the hype around personal budgets makes way for a more mature debate about how to achieve personalisation in a deeper, more meaningful way; and as current work continues to place user involvement at the heart of service reform through user-led organisations and peer networks, perhaps *Personalisation through Participation* holds the key for the future. As we suggested back in 2004: 'once you start personalising public services people will get an appetite for it. They will want more.'

15 A house of experiment

Demos and the politics of science

James Wilsdon

In the summer of 2003, two significant dates were marked in the Demos diary. The first was our tenth birthday. In anticipation of this milestone, the Demos team underwent one of our periodic bursts of introspection, which resulted in a new strapline ('people changing politics'), a revamped set of research themes, and a fresh way of describing ourselves to the wider world (as 'a greenhouse for new ideas').

This idea of a think-tank as 'greenhouse' reflected broader Demos concerns around openness and transparency, and influenced our decision to make all our publications open access under the Creative Commons licensing system (at the time, Demos was the first UK think-tank to go down this route). We marked our birthday by digitising and releasing our entire archive, both online and (in a move that already seems decidedly quaint) by handing out boxfuls of 'a decade of Demos on a disc'.

The other big event of summer 2003 was the Progressive Governance conference, the annual schmoozefest for centre-left leaders and thinkers, which Tony Blair hosted on a grand scale in London that July. Bill Clinton, Thabo Mbeki, Luiz Inácio Lula da Silva and Helen Clark topped the bill, and 600 participants from forty countries took part.

The conference was originally conceived as a celebration of the international reach of 'third way' thinking, but these ambitions had been derailed by the decision to invade Iraq in March 2003, and the fierce debate that this provoked on the left and among the wider public. As a result, the conference had an uneasy air: like a party where the Blairite hardcore were determined to keep dancing, even though the music had stopped and the house lights had been switched back on.

Demos wasn't one of the organisers of the conference – Peter Mandelson and Policy Network were firmly in the driving seat – but Tom Bentley (then Demos' Director) and I were asked to draft two of the policy papers that framed the agenda.

With controversies over genetically modified (GM) crops and the measles, mumps and rubella (MMR) vaccine still fresh in people's minds, my paper (co-authored with Rebecca Willis, who at the time was Director of Green Alliance) took technology, risk and the environment as its theme. It reflected on lessons from GM and MMR for the development and diffusion of other emerging technologies. We took nanotechnologies as a particular focus: a fast-growing research field ripe with scientific, technological and economic potential, but where recent critical noises from, among others, Prince Charles, Bill Joy (the cofounder of Sun Microsystems) and a handful of environmental groups had led some to predict that it could become 'the next GM'.

Our paper sketched a path between uncritical technophilia (displayed at times by New Labour), and the outright rejection of certain technologies by the green and anti-globalisation movements. 'How', we asked, 'can the potential of new technologies be harnessed to wider projects of economic and social renewal without giving rise to such negative and polarised responses? Are there new approaches to the development and diffusion of new technologies that are more responsive to social and ethical concerns, and can move the site of public debate further upstream within research and development processes?'

It was an example of Demos doing what it often does best: acting as an intermediary between the worlds of academia and policy, by providing a digestible summary of arguments which scholars (in this case, those working on the sociology of risk and in science and technology studies) had made over recent years. It was a topical theme: the following year, these issues would receive a more detailed treatment in *The Death of Environmentalism*, by the US environmentalists Ted Nordhaus and Michael Shellenberger, which led to the creation of the Breakthrough Institute, and provoked a debate about green attitudes towards new technologies which continues to rage today (for example, in George Monbiot's support for nuclear power, or recent remarks by the green campaigner Mark Lynas in support of GM crops).

The novelty of the Demos work was in elaborating the idea of 'upstream public engagement', a phrase that Brian Wynne, a sociologist of science, had used in a couple of academic papers, but which had not yet found its way into the policy discourse. The idea was simple: rather than waiting for new technologies to be so advanced that development and commercialisation trajectories were fixed (which was arguably one of the causes of public disquiet over GM crops and foods) the locus of public engagement should move 'upstream' so that broader dialogue and debate could help to inform the direction of funding and policy for research and innovation.

This was also the only time I've benefited from prime ministerial peer review. Having circulated a first draft, we were surprised to receive a three-page handwritten commentary from Tony Blair, written as he modestly put it 'from the perspective of a policymaker grappling with these issues'. He touched on lessons from MMR, and conceded that:

In respect of issues like GM, it is possible to proceed more deliberatively. But it needs real public engagement and it needs the science to be more accessible. Unless it becomes so, even the most 'public' debate can be a mixture of the dedicated, the expert and the cranky.

Encouraged by the reception for this paper, we decided to write a fuller account of the case for upstream public engagement, which Demos published as *See-through Science* in 2004.[1] This prompted a supportive editorial in *Nature*,[2] and sparked interest (and some opposition) from science bodies, research councils and policy makers in the UK and further afield. We even managed to get the phrase 'upstream engagement' included in Gordon Brown's 10-Year *Framework for Science and Innovation*, which was published that same year.

At the time, Demos was piloting various ways of moving ideas from policy to practice, and had growing streams of research and consultancy in education, the arts, social care and local government. We decided to attempt the same for science, and in late 2004 I switched roles in Demos (from head of strategy) to lead this new programme.

See-through Science became the first in a series of Demos projects on the politics of science and technology, which together amounted to a substantial body of work (including *The Public Value of Science* (2005), *Better Humans?* (2005) *Governing at the Nanoscale* (2006), *The Received Wisdom* (2006) and *The Slow Race* (2006). We also facilitated several public engagement exercises (including *Nanodialogues* (2007)), and broadened our international scope to analyse science and innovation policy in emerging economies (through the series of *Atlas of Ideas* studies on China, India, Brazil and South Korea, which Charlie Leadbeater and I coordinated from 2006 to 2008).

It can be hard for think-tanks to claim responsibility for particular impacts, given that their role is often to diffuse and persuade others to take ownership of ideas. But, couched in all the usual caveats, I think Demos' science programme had an influence in the following ways. First, it helped to build a consensus among UK science policy makers and research councils that public engagement had a constructive role to play. This unlocked new sources of funding (for example, the Sciencewise programme) and encouraged a flowering of public dialogue exercises which continue today, particularly in emerging fields like synthetic biology and geoengineering, where the notion of 'upstream engagement' remains helpful.

Second, Demos helped to open up science and innovation policy to more diverse voices. Ten years ago, the field was largely the preserve of research funders and learned societies (with a handful of academic centres like SPRU at Sussex University and PREST at Manchester University). None of the mainstream political think-tanks worked on these issues. Now, the terrain is far noisier and more contested, with new players like Nesta and Will Hutton's Big Innovation Centre challenging traditional accounts of innovation policy, and a host of organisations – large and small – regularly piling into debates over science funding, communication and the social dilemmas raised by new technologies. Demos played an important part in this shift.

Third, through *The Atlas of Ideas*, Demos made a contribution to debates over the globalisation of science and innovation, and prompted UK policy makers to develop more sophisticated strategies for collaboration with China, India and Brazil. The value of those reports is reflected in the fact that Nesta, the Foreign Office and the Research Councils have recently updated our analysis of India, and are now doing the same for China.

Finally, on a more personal note, it changed the direction of my own career. When writing *See-through Science* we were very taken by the work of the US sociologist Stephen Hilgartner, who described expert scientific advice as a form of performance. In the pamphlet, we had some fun playing around with theatrical metaphors. The context at the time was a landmark Royal Society report on the social and environmental impacts of nanotechnologies, which had just been published.

We described how, unusually, this study had relied on an ensemble cast. On the Royal Society's working group, alongside the usual principals – eminent Fellows in physics, medicine and engineering, the head of a Cambridge college and a senior industrialist – were some unexpected supporting players – an environmentalist, a social scientist and a consumer champion. It was also imaginatively staged. Aspects of the Royal Society's performance were carefully rehearsed, but there was also room for improvisation. It consulted widely, ran workshops with stakeholders, and published evidence on its website. And it was deliberately avant-garde. Anyone familiar with the Royal Society's earlier work could spot that its tone was unusually precautionary. Social and ethical issues received prominent billing. Uncertainty and dialogue were recurring motifs.

Little did I know that four years later, I would end up joining the troupe, when I moved on from Demos to become director of science policy at the Royal Society. Historian of science Stephen Shapin has written eloquently about the Royal Society's origins in the 17th century as a 'house of experiment'.[3] These days, no scientific experiments take place within the walls of its elegant home in Carlton House Terrace. But experiments of other kinds continue all the time at the boundaries between science, society, politics and policy. Some succeed; others produce messy, even explosive, reactions. For a few years, I'm proud that Demos managed to create a house of experiment of its own.

Notes

1 Wilsdon J and Willis R *See-through Science: Why public engagement needs to move upstream,* London: Demos, 2004.

2 'Going public', Nature, 431, 2004, p 883, available at: www.nature.com/nature/journal/v431/n7011/full/431883a.html (accessed 15 July 2013)

3 Shapin S, *Never Pure: Historical Studies of Science as if It Was Produced by People with Bodies, Situated in Time, Space, Culture and Society, and Struggling for Credibility and Authority,* Johns Hopkins University Press: Baltimore, MD, 2010.

16 Character (revisited)

Why parents are the principal architects of a fairer society

Richard Reeves

One of the things I enjoyed most about my time at Demos was that internal arguments were often as fierce as the external ones. There was certainly a robust debate in Demos HQ when we launched a strand of work on the question of character. For some, 'character' was a quasi-religious concern best left to social conservatives. Attributing social problems – even problems for progressives like inequality – to character steers dangerously close to 'blaming the victim'. It can seem a short step from identifying the contribution of particular character attributes to life chances, to laying responsibility solely at the door of the individual.

This danger is real. But it is outweighed, in my view, by the opposite danger: turning a blind eye to the evidence linking character and opportunity, and thereby failing to address a major cause of inequality. This is difficult ethical, political and operational territory for policy makers. But there is also something morally awry when affluent opinion-formers strive to build character in their own children, knowing its importance for their prospects – but then deny its wider significance.

What drove us, in 2009, to delve into the question of character was the growing evidence that certain character strengths (or I could say 'attributes', 'traits', 'capabilities', 'virtues', 'skills' – there is a lively academic argument raging on this, believe me) are closely linked to social mobility. Work by Julia Margo, then at IPPR, but shortly to join Demos, had already shown the increased predictive power of what Nobel-prize winner James Heckman labelled 'non-cognitive skills'.

Particularly important are the ability to defer gratification, or prudence; the capacity to stick with difficult, often unrewarding tasks, often labelled 'grit' or perseverance; and productivity, or industriousness. In addition, an ability to work with others – empathy, or 'social skill' – is strongly related to life chances.

After some organisational soul-searching, Jen Lexmond and I produced an analysis, published as *Building Character*, showing a powerful influence of parenting style and quality on character formation even in the pre-school years. At the same time, the Demos *Character Inquiry* was launched. Jen and I found, in line with other studies, that quality of parenting was a more important predictor of certain child outcomes than income. In fact, once parenting quality was taken into account, income in and of itself was not significantly linked to character development. David Cameron MP, then Leader of the Opposition, spoke at the launch event. His assessment of the *Building Character* research result was positive. 'It would be over the top to say that it is to social science what *E=MC2* was to physics' he declared. 'But it is one of the most important findings for a generation.' Well, it got us some headlines.

I think it would be fair to say that Mr Cameron's interest in character was overtaken by events. Five months after making his speech he was in Government, in coalition with Nick Clegg (my next boss, after Demos) and facing grave economic circumstances. (Indeed, one of the small tragedies of David Cameron is that he reinvented the Conservative party along social lines – including greater interest in issue such as character, social value, parenting, social capital – but has ended up leading a government up to its elbows in economics.)

Nonetheless, the question of character and its relation to inequality continues to be asked, both in the UK and in my new home, the United States. Almost unnoticed by the media, the Independent Riots Communities and Victims Panel concluded in 2012, as follows:

In asking what it was that made young people make the right choice in the heat of the moment, the Panel heard of the importance of character... A number of attributes together form character, including self-discipline, application, the ability to defer gratification, and resilience in recovering from setbacks. Young people who develop character will be best-placed to make the most of their lives.

More recently, the All Party Parliamentary Group on Social Mobility has highlighted the role of character 'as the missing link in mobility – a force at play throughout the lifecycle but all too often overlooked in favour of more tangible, easier-to-measure factors.' The APPG has hosted a summit on character and resilience and is continuing to work in this area.

On the other side of the Atlantic, there is a renewed interest in the issue of character, sparked in part by an excellent book by Paul Tough – *How Children Succeed: Grit, Curiosity and the Hidden Power of Character.* Tough is no conservative: his background and motivation is in poverty and disadvantage. His book marshals the evidence for the links between character and mobility: from chess clubs in Harlem to tests for West Point military recruits, the data all point one way.

Liberals are realising, often with a degree of discomfort, that a meritocratic society has to create not only opportunities, *but also people who can seize them.* Character development is slowly, but surely, becoming an egalitarian concern.

Motivation is important here. For me, character is an issue for policy because of the evidence that character is a factor for opportunity. This is about fairness, not goodness. It is not a moral question, except to the extent that equality of opportunity is a moral question. That is also the motivation of Paul Tough, James Heckman (the godfather of character studies), Angela Duckworth and Yvonne Roberts, all researching in this field. It is certainly the motivation of Jen Lexmond, who now, among other activities, heads Character Counts (*www.charactercountsgroup.org*).

Far from signalling a retreat for government in general or for social policy in particular, the identification of character as an ingredient for mobility signals a new approach from government: one focused as much on the development of character for the long run, as on the amelioration of immediate material disadvantage.

Policy matters, because character can be deliberately shaped and reshaped. It is not fixed, inscribed on our souls at birth. Character is malleable. As Tough writes: 'The character strengths that matter so much to children's success are not innate; they don't appear in us magically, as a result of good luck or good genes. And they are not simply a choice. They are rooted in brain chemistry, and they are molded, in measurable and predictable ways, by the environment in which children grow up'.

A focus on character, then, does not replace the need to address poverty: it simply broadens our ambitions. In a sense, we are going back full circle, to Aristotle and his views on the creation of a good society. It turns out that the title of his greatest work might have been better translated not as the *Ethics*, but as *On Character*. No surprise that character sounds like an old idea. No surprise either that, all too often, it has been monopolised by conservatives. But in the hands of modern liberals, character is – ought to be – a force for progress and equality.

17 Building the service nation

A blueprint for the future of civic service

Sonia Sodha

Little did we realise when we embarked on a Demos project on citizen service in 2009 that it would end in a ministerial apology to the NUS, some ruffled shadow ministerial feathers and a bemused Sky news reporter grilling a Demos researcher with: 'so, let's just get this straight – you're proposing to charge university students more to pay for them to do compulsory community service?'

The idea of national civic service – a community-based rite of passage to take the place formerly held by national military service – has obvious political appeal. Back in 2009 it was clear it was going to play a major role in the party manifestos. David Cameron had made a summer service scheme for 16-year-olds the flagship of his Big Society agenda, and Gordon Brown announced the Labour manifesto would include a requirement all young people do 50 hours of community service by the time they turned 19.

The Labour MP Frank Field wrote an article for *Prospect* advocating a compulsory year-long citizen service scheme for all 18-year-olds. The high level of political interest in the idea – but a certain amount of muddiness in the policy debate about what the various iterations of these schemes were going to achieve, and a lack of consultation with young people about what they thought – was the context in which we decided to undertake the Demos research on citizen service, supported by the Private Equity Foundation.

Our report, *Service Nation*, started off by asking: if citizen service is the answer, what is the question? Service tends to be held up as a 'silver bullet' policy in the context of a depressingly problem-based analysis: our young people need more discipline; the education system doesn't prepare them properly for work; we're too diffuse a society, with people living parallel lives; there's too much of a 'get-rich-quick', celebrity-obsessed culture.

Because it is a neat solution with widespread popular appeal, the temptation has always been to jump straight from this broad-brush social commentary to prescribing some form of citizen service to cure all social ills. Too often, this happens without asking the hard questions: why would a compulsory year-long scheme help with employability, given that many places would be poor quality due to the numbers involved? Why would 50 hours of compulsory volunteering while of school age boost youth engagement if there's no connection to what they're learning about citizenship? Would doing a two-week residential course at the age of 16 with young people from different social backgrounds really promote more social mixing, when participants come from and return to divided communities?

Our research started from the belief that to understand what form of youth civic service government should be promoting, we needed a deeper interrogation of what gaps it could fill; a hard-headed look at the evidence on what has been effective; and a conversation with young people about their views.

The example of 17-year-old Paris Brown, the first youth police and crime commissioner, helps to illuminate the difficulties young people in Britain currently face. Earlier this year, she wept her way through a public apology for a series of offensive tweets sent when she was younger, following her resignation after a Daily Mail exposé. Our society expects children to behave like mini-adults as soon as they're able to create a social media profile, holds them responsible for crimes from the age of 10 and blasts them with sophisticated advertising and inappropriate sexual images.

Young people are also increasingly required to carve their own path through a difficult labour market: traditional apprenticeships and jobs-for-life have become rarer, and while numbers going to university have grown exponentially, it is predominantly middle-class young people who get to experience this educational and social transition.

In this context, there is an important question about how we help bridge young people's transitions to adulthood and support them to build the character capabilities, mindset and social skills they need to navigate the modern world. All young people – not just those going to university – deserve not just to be set high expectations in terms of what they can contribute and achieve, but also to have access to structured opportunities that help them develop.

There also remains uncertainty about what it means to be a citizen of modern Britain. The Conservatives never really succeeded in lifting Big Society off the page of their 2010 manifesto, the optimistically titled *Invitation to Join the Government of Britain*. It failed to move beyond a vague call to arms. Yet Big Society did tap into an instinct many people share: we are not a particularly cohesive society, and there is huge untapped value in people's time, especially in forming relationships across social boundaries, whether that be through volunteer reading help in schools, mentoring young people or spending time with isolated older people. Where Big Society missed a trick, however, was in failing to realise that people want and need structured ways in which they can make a contribution.

Our recommendations for citizen service started from three key principles. First, if service is about building a more integrated, active citizenry it cannot be boiled down to a one-shot, compulsory scheme that young people are shoehorned into at some point between the ages of 16 to 18. If we are really serious about influencing culture, norms and behaviour, it needs to start earlier, with younger children at primary school. Second, that to be meaningful, service has to be focused on outcomes – the 'double benefit' of developing young people while at the same time making a difference to communities. And third, service should be reserved neither for a 'problem' type of young person nor affluent gap years: it should be a leveller that draws on all types of talent and experience.

This led us to recommend a life-cycle approach to service, spanning primary school to retirement, but particularly focusing on children and young people. To foster a culture of service in young people, we recommended that schools should deliver US-style 'service learning' as part of the curriculum, which is very different both to classroom-based citizenship and a tacked-on requirement for volunteering hours. Through service learning, children undertake team-based community projects that are linked to academic goals and reflection in the classroom. This type of experiential 'learning by doing' requires children to solve complex problems in real-world settings and promotes skills like teamwork and community involvement, and in the US functions as a pipeline for the AmeriCorps full-time youth service scheme.

We recommended this should lead onto a range of more structured service experiences, ranging from opportunities to take part in full-time service as part of compulsory 16–18 education; gap-year style full-time service opportunities; and expansion of schemes like TeachFirst within education and to other areas like social work and youth work, with a focus on sustainable expansion of high-quality schemes that benefit both young people and the community. We thought the Conservatives' suggested scheme should sit within this broader range of opportunities.

In order to stress that service is something for all young people, and that those who benefit the most have an obligation to 'give back', we also suggested that university undergraduates could be required to undertake a modest amount of community service in exchange for the state subsidy of their university education (back in 2009, roughly £8,000 per year). And to stress that provision of full-time service opportunities is about supporting *all* young people into adulthood and employment, that it would be equitable to fund an expansion of service opportunities by introducing an interest rate of 2.5 per cent on student maintenance loans, up from 0 per cent in 2009 (much to the bewilderment of the Sky News reporter).

There have been exciting developments in the four years since we wrote the report. The Government has launched its NCS scheme, involving a two-week residential course and 30 hours spent working on a community action project. As we recommended, the Government is looking at how to embed it within a broader lifecycle approach: the Prime Minister commissioned Dame Julia Cleverdon and Amanda Jordan to undertake an independent review of how government can help establish a decade of social action opportunities for young people aged between 10 and 20 which was launched this summer by the Prince of Wales, with cross-party support. TeachFirst has expanded, and a social work equivalent, Frontline, has recently been set up.

There are now more gap-year style structured service opportunities available, although demand far outstrips supply. City Year, the programme that helped spawn AmeriCorps in the US, has now, with philanthropic and business support, set up in London, and will be available in Birmingham from next year. It places 18 – 25 year-olds from a diverse range of backgrounds in deprived inner-city schools for a year, where they run breakfast and after-school clubs, provide one-to-one tutoring, and act as mentors. They benefit from 300 hours of professional training and development, including from its business partners. In the US, where the scheme has been around for over 25 years, its corporate supporters often recruit scheme alumni because of the skills it develop.

There are four priorities for building on this solid base. The first must be on developing the role of the school system in service and social action, both because of its importance in getting children excited about the potential of service when they are young, and because of the benefits it can bring for their learning if done well.

Second, the number of full-time service places offered through schemes like CityYear remains small. It needs to grow organically, led by the youth social action sector, but there are important changes government can make to support this. Some are relatively simple, like clarifying the status of full-time service programmes in relation to minimum wage legislation.

Service schemes also have huge potential in terms of youth unemployment: funding a service year for long-term NEETs as a way of boosting employability. For example, the Labour party could incorporate it as part of its youth jobs guarantee: rather than fund 25 hours a week of work in a minimum wage job, why not fund a £100 a week stipend in a high-quality, full-time service opportunity that builds young people's contacts with potential employers and gives them real skills?

Third, where service has been successful elsewhere in the world, it has been because of a partnership between the voluntary and community sector, the private sector and government. Politicians from all parties have talked about the responsibility businesses have to young people, for example in providing apprenticeship opportunities. The Labour party has even said it would limit eligibility for public procurement contracts to those businesses offering apprenticeships. Why not expand that to companies who support charities providing high-quality service opportunities?

Fourth, the debate has very much been one about youth citizen service. A genuinely life-cycle approach to service would see structured opportunities being available to people throughout their working lives and into retirement.

An aim of City Year is that one day, the question 'where are you going to do your service year?' will be as common as 'what are you going to do after school?' We may be a long way off that here in the UK. But as university becomes more expensive, as many employers seem of the view that it doesn't adequately prepare young people for the workplace anyway, and as there seems to be a growing consensus that while society isn't broken, many of us would like to live in a society in which we all contribute more, service has the potential to be a different sort of rite of passage to work and to citizenship for our young people.

18 Do something different

The role of an entrepreneurial state in fostering innovation

Mariana Mazzucato[1]

...our disability is discursive: we simply do not know how to talk about things anymore.

Tony Judt, *Ill Fares the Land*

The state is attacked and increasingly dismantled, through images of its bureaucratic, inertial, heavy-handed character. While innovation is not the state's main role, illustrating its potential innovative and dynamic character – its historical ability, in some countries, to play an *entrepreneurial* role in society – is perhaps the most effective way to defend its existence, and size.

I wrote the Demos pamphlet *The Entrepreneurial State* in the manner of the political '*pamflets*' of the 1800s: quickly, out of a sense of *urgency*. I wanted to convince the UK government to change strategy: to not cut state programmes in the name of making the economy 'more competitive' and more 'entrepreneurial', but to reimagine what the state *can* and must do to ensure a sustainable post-crisis recovery. Highlighting the active role that the state *has* played in the 'hotbeds' of innovation and entrepreneurship – like Silicon Valley – was the key to showing that the state can not only facilitate the knowledge economy, but actively create it with a bold vision and targeted investment.

The pamphlet made strong waves in the UK, with attention from Rt. Hon David Willetts MP (Secretary of State, BIS), who cited it in two speeches,[2] Lord Heseltine (who included its contents in his Review), and Chuka Umunna MP (Shadow Business Secretary), who, after asking for the contents to be presented to him personally, as well as to his team, has taken it on board to define his 'Active State' agenda. In the Netherlands, the Minister of Economic Affairs Henk Kamp requested the key points from the pamphlet be presented by me to his ministry (200 audience), and the presentation later appeared on a two page spread of the national paper NRC.[3] And UK journalists have written about it such as the piece by Anthony Hilton in The Independent who perfectly summarised the key point: *Europe should not do what the US says it does but what it actually does.*[4]

Indeed, the same title could today apply to Greece and Germany. So much of Germany's success is due to its (public) spending on R&D, directing that spending in visionary mission-oriented new directions (green), its publicly funded Fraunhofer Institutes that enable dynamic science-industry links, and the state funded 'patient' finance through the German state investment bank KfW. Instead the German medicine to Greece is: 'do as we did, tighten your belts'.[5]

I have since written a follow-up book on *The Entrepreneurial State* for Anthem Press, which was recently published, and infamously called 'heretical' in a very positive review in Forbes.[6] This significantly expanded version of the Demos pamphlet builds on that initial research and pushes it harder, drawing out further implications at the firm and sectoral level. One chapter, dedicated entirely to Apple Inc., looks at the whole span of state support that this leading 'new economy' company has received.

After looking at the role of the state in making the most courageous investments behind the internet and IT revolution two chapters look at the next big thing: 'green' technology. Unsurprisingly we find that across the globe the countries leading in the green revolution (solar and wind energy are the paradigmatic examples explored) are those where the state is playing an active role beyond that which is typically attributed to market failure theory. And the public sector organizations involved, such as development banks in Brazil and China, are not just providing countercyclical lending (as Keynes would have asked for), but even 'directing' that lending towards the most innovative parts of the 'green' economy.

Questions about whether such 'directionality' should raise the usual worries about the state's inability to 'pick winners' are confronted head-on – demystifying old assumptions. The new book also looks more explicitly at the collective group of actors that are required to create innovation-led growth and questions whether the current innovation 'ecosystem' is a functional *symbiotic* one or a dysfunctional *parasitic* one. Can a unconfident state even recognise the difference? The last two chapters of the book go deeper into this question by asking how we can make sure that the distribution of the returns (rewards) generated from active state investments in innovation are just as social as the risks taken. Indeed, some of the very criticisms that have recently been directed at the banks (socialisation of risk, privatisation of rewards) appear to be just as relevant in the 'real' innovation economy.

The reason I call, both the Demos report and the Anthem book, the 'entrepreneurial' state is that entrepreneurship – what every policy maker today seems to want to encourage – is not (just) about start-ups, venture capital and 'garage tinkerers'. It is about the willingness and ability of economic agents to take on risk and real *Knightian* uncertainty: what is genuinely unknown.[7]

Attempts at innovation usually fail – otherwise it would not be called 'innovation'. This is why you have to be a bit 'crazy' to engage with innovation... it will often cost you more than it brings back, making traditional cost–benefit analysis stop it from the start. But whereas Steve Jobs talked about this in his charismatic 2005 Stanford lecture on the need for innovators to stay 'hungry and foolish', few have admitted how much such foolishness has been 'seriously' riding on the wave of state-funded and -directed innovations.

The state 'foolishly' developing innovations? Yes, most of the radical, revolutionary innovations that have fuelled the dynamics of capitalism – from railroads to the internet, to modern-day nanotechnology and pharmaceuticals – trace the most courageous early and capital-intensive 'entrepreneurial' investments back to the state. And, as is argued fully in the book, all of the technologies that make Jobs' iPhone so 'smart' were government funded (internet, GPS, touch-screen display and the recent SIRI voice activated personal assistant). Such radical investments did not come about due to the presence of venture capitalists. Nor 'garage tinkerers'. It was the visible hand of the state that made these innovations happen. Innovation that would not have come about had we waited for the 'market' and business to do it alone – or government to simply stand aside and provide the basics.

But how have economists talked about this? They have either ignored it or talked about it in terms of the state simply fixing 'market failures'. Standard economic theory justifies state intervention when the social return on investment is higher than the private return – making it unlikely that a private business will invest. This applies from cleaning up pollution (a negative 'externality' not included in companies' costs) to funding basic research (a 'public good' difficult to appropriate). Yet this explains less than one-quarter of the R&D investments made in the USA. Big visionary projects – like putting 'a man on the moon', or creating the vision behind the internet and modern-day nanotechnology – required much more than the calculation of social and private returns.

Such challenges required a vision, a mission, and most of all *confidence* about what the state's role in the economy is. As eloquently argued by Keynes in the *The End of Laissez Faire* (1926), 'The important thing for Government is not to do things which individuals are doing already, and to do them a little better or a little worse; but to do those things which at present are not done at all.' Such a task requires vision and the desire to *make things happen* in specific spaces – requiring not just bureaucratic skills but real technology-specific and sector-specific expertise.

It is only through an exciting vision of the state's role that such expertise can be recruited, and able to then map out the landscape in the relevant space. Indeed, a key part of DARPA's 'secret' – the agency that invented *and* commercialised the internet within the US Department of Defense – has been its ability to attract talent and create excitement around specific missions. And it is no coincidence that a similar agency in today's US Department of Energy, ARPA-E, is not only leading US green investments, but also having fun on the way (welcoming the trial and error process in energy research rather than fearing it) and attracting great brains in energy research.

While many of the examples in the book come from the US – purposely to show how the country that is often argued to most represent the benefits of the 'free-market system' has one of the most interventionist governments when it comes to innovation – modern-day examples are coming more from 'emerging' countries. Visionary investments are exemplified today by confident state investment banks in countries like Brazil and China – not only providing countercyclical lending but also *directing* that lending to new uncertain areas that private banks and venture capitalists (VCs) fear. And here too, like in DARPA, expertise, talent and vision matter.

Equally, it is state investment banks (in Brazil, China, Germany) that are today providing the scaled up *patient* capital to the green economy. In China, the China Development Bank that is today leading the country's investments in the green economy. While the usual suspects worry that these public banks 'crowd out' private lending, the truth is that these banks are operating in sectors, and particular areas within these sectors, that the private banks fear. It is about the state acting as a force for innovation and change, not only 'de-risking' risk-averse private actors, but also boldly leading the way, with a clear and courageous vision – exactly the opposite image of the state that is usually sold.

And this is the punch line: when organised effectively, the state's hand is firm but not heavy, providing the vision and the dynamic *push* (as well as some 'nudges' – though nudges don't get you the IT revolution of the past, nor the green revolution today) to make things happen that otherwise would not have. Such actions are meant to increase the courage of private business. This requires understanding the state as neither a 'meddler' nor a simple 'facilitator' of economic growth. It is a key partner of the private sector – and often a more daring one, willing to take the risks that business won't.

The state cannot and should not bow down easily to interest groups who approach it to seek handouts, rents and unnecessary privileges like tax cuts. It should seek instead for those interest groups to work dynamically with it in its search for growth and technological change. Indeed, when not confident, it is more likely that the state will get 'captured' and bow to private interests. When not taking a leading role, the state becomes a poor imitator of private sector behaviours, rather than a real alternative. And the usual criticisms of the state as slow and bureaucratic are more likely in countries that sideline it to play a purely 'administrative' role.

So it is a self-fulfilling prophecy to treat the state as cumbersome, and only able to correct 'market failures'. Who would want to work in the state sector if that is how it is described? And is it a coincidence that the 'picking winners' problem – the fear that the state is unable to make bold decisions on the *direction* of change – is discussed especially in countries that don't have an entrepreneurial vision for the state, i.e. countries where the state takes a backseat and is then blamed as soon as it makes a mistake? Major socioeconomic 'challenges' such as climate change and 'ageing' require an active state, making the need for a better understanding of its role within public–private partnerships more important than ever.

Providing such leadership, the state makes things happen that otherwise would not have. A confident government recognizes fully that the business sector might 'talk' about tax but 'walks' to where new technological and market opportunities are – and that this is strongly correlated with areas characterized by major public sector investments. Did Pfizer recently leave Sandwich in Kent to go to Boston in the US due to the latter's lower tax and lower regulation? Or was it due to the fact that the public sector National Institutes of Health (NIH) have been spending close to $32 billion per year in the USA funding the knowledge base on which private pharmaceutical firms thrive?

In economics, the 'crowding-out' hypothesis is used to analyse the possibility that increased state spending reduces private business investment, since both compete for the same pool of savings (through borrowing), which might then result in higher interest rates which reduces the willingness of private firms to borrow, and hence invest. While Keynesian analysis has argued against this possibility during periods of under-utilised capacity, the point is that *even in the boom* (when in theory there is full capacity utilisation), there are in practice many parts of the risk landscape where private business fears to tread, with government leading the way. In fact, the spending that led to the internet occurred mainly during boom times – as was the government spending that lead to the nanotechnology industry.

Thus a proper defence of the state should argue that it not only 'crowds in' private investment (by increasing GDP through the multiplier effect) – a correct but limited point made by Keynesians – it does something more. Crowding in is a concept that – while defending the public sector – is still using as a benchmark the negative: the possibility that government investment crowds out private investment, by competing for the same limited amount of savings. If we want to describe something positive and visionary, a word that is bolder and offensive, not defensive, should be used.

Rather than analysing the state's active role through its correction of 'market failures' (emphasised by many 'progressive' economists who rightly see many failures), it is necessary to build a theory of the state's role in *shaping* and *creating* markets – more in line with the work of Karl Polanyi who emphasized how the capitalist 'market' has from the start been heavily shaped by state actions. In innovation, the state not only 'crowds in' business investment but also 'dynamises' it in – creating the vision, the mission and the plan.

Notes

1 This chapter is adapted from the Introduction of my new book on *The Entrepreneurial State: debunking private vs. public sector myths,* published by Anthem Press, www.anthempress.com/the-entrepreneurial-state.

2 David Willetts, 'Our High Tech Future', 2012, available at: www.bis.gov.uk/news/speeches/davidwilletts- policy-exchange-britain-best-place-science-2012. David Willetts, Bernal Lecture, 2012, available at: www.bbk.ac.uk/events-calendar/bernal-lecture-2012.

3 Van der Heijden M, An entrepreneurial, innovative state' (translation of: Een ondernemende staat, dÍe innoveert), *NRC Weekend Zaterdag*, 2013, p 4–5.

4 Hilton A, 'To be more like Americans, Europe should do what they do, not what they say they do', *The Independent*, 25 February 2012.

5 For an elaboration of this argument, and the relevance of The Entrepreneurial State for the Eurozone, see my article in Euromove, October 2012, http://ymlp.com/zm2bu9.

6 Upbin B, 'Debunking the narrative of Silicon Valley's innovation might', Forbes, 2013, available at: www.forbes.com/sites/bruceupbin/2013/06/13/ debunking-the-narrative-of-silicon-valleys-innovation-might.

7 Knightian uncertainty' refers to the 'immeasurable' risk, i.e. a risk that cannot be calculated. This economic concept is named after University of Chicago economist Frank Knight (1885–1972), who theorized about risk and uncertainty and their differences in economic terms.

19 The map and the territory

Better understanding the creative industries can help in the quest for growth

Helen Burrows

What role might the creative industries play in promoting that elusive goal of economic growth? With our 2011 report *Risky Business*, Kitty Ussher and I hoped to shine a light on a sector that had great growth potential, but was surprisingly poorly understood.

The creative industries, which include advertising, architecture, art and antiques, fashion, film and video, music, the performing arts, publishing, software, television and radio, as well as other sectors, account for more than ten per cent of the UK's exports. Growth in employment in the creative economy is five times that of the rest of the economy. Clearly, the sector has an important part to play in economic and employment recovery, yet it has faced long standing policy challenges, particularly in its ability to access finance.

So we set out to take a fresh look at the creative industries and provide the missing comparative analysis between it and other sectors of the economy.

Our findings challenged some commonly held assumptions about the creative industries.

First, there are no more small businesses in it than in any other sector of the economy. Second, when we looked at the sector as a whole, the survival rate is on trend with the rest of the economy, and notably lower than in other sectors frequently described as 'risky' such as hotels and catering. These two findings taken together challenged the commonly held perceptions that the creative industries are 'different' or 'riskier' than other sectors of the economy.

Of course, business survival is not the same as business success, and aggregate outcomes do not mean that there is no, or less risk in the creative industries than elsewhere in the economy. Rather, we argued that the sector is better understood as one where, as elsewhere in the economy, there is a range from the highly risky and unpredictable (for example, creating new content such as films, TV, music or games) to lower risk and more stable (for example, an agency model where creative work is carried out on commission).

Our third finding was that a lack of good quality data on the creative industries is a driver of these misunderstandings, and we made the case for both public and private sector action to address this. As Risky Business discussed in its fourth chapter, The Map, 'there can be no economic analysis without classification': good quality, regularly reported, granular data, analysed by a range of experts, is the key to understanding any sector of the economy, and the businesses within it.

The system of international Standard Industrial Classification (SIC) codes for collecting and sorting economic data that the Office for National Statistics (ONS) uses has its origins in the great depression of the 1930s. Then, the Government realised that it didn't know what was going on in the economy and was therefore in a poor position to develop policies to enable growth. The SIC system was developed in response to this and introduced in 1948.

Despite gradual updates, it has changed little since. This means that historically significant economic sectors such as manufacturing and agriculture are well served by the classification system we use today while newer sectors, including the creative industries, are not. For example, in the current system there are 281 detailed codes covering the manufacturing sector, but only 49 that are relevant to the creative industries, as defined by the Department of Culture, Media and Sport (DCMS).

Indeed, the very fact that the DCMS has become involved in the classification of the creative industries is a response to the inadequacy of the current SIC system – the activity, trends and patterns in creative industries are 'lost' within the data sets used elsewhere in Whitehall, most obviously in the data sets used by analysts at the Treasury and Department for Business, Innovation and Skills (BIS).

We found that this has a double impact, in that most private sector economic analysis follows the example of the SIC system, and therefore repeats its mistakes, leaving the creative industries also underreported by private analysts. Research published by BIS at around the same time found similar issues – describing 'asymmetry of information' between creative businesses and their potential financiers as a cause of the ongoing market failure in investment. Therefore, the need for better quality data in order to encourage private sector investment is clear.

So what is the way ahead? The attempt in 2011 by the DCMS to tweak how the sector was measured ran into some trouble, both due to some sub-sectors such as music being miscategorised or receiving varying levels of detail, and because some of the fastest growing businesses, such as Shazam, Spotify, ASOS and Netaporter, were too dynamic to fit into existing definitions. This controversy led to the Creative Industries Council (CIC) setting up the Technical Working Group chaired by Hasan Bakhshi and Jeremy Silver (on which I also sit) to look at the issues.

Progress is being made, firstly in agreeing a logical definition of a creative business, using 'creative intensity' to assess the proportion of creative jobs in an industry. There is also potential to reform the existing 'map', both through establishing and improving 'bottom up' data collection by the sector itself and pressing for change to the international SIC system.

In terms of broader changes, a White Paper on Communications has been anticipated since early 2012, while the passage of the Communications Data Bill has run into trouble. Some reasons for these difficulties, such as the Leveson process and the politics of the coalition, are obvious, but there may be a deeper, machinery of Government challenge here.

In *Risky Business* we showed that the very structure of Government departments mirrors the categorisation of the economy drawn up in the 1930s, described above. The issues new communications legislation must address, on data, privacy and security are important, complex, and pressing. Unfortunately they currently cut across the agendas of several departments, including DCMS, BIS and the Home Office.

While the attack in Woolwich might have reignited the debate over the Communications Data Bill, a bigger issue for the long-term is the large technology companies' self-image as part of our democracy as well as our economy: similar to the printing press before them.

While there is truth in this, we must remember that the first priority of these businesses is delivering value to (international) shareholders, not nurturing British or international democracy, security, nor looking after intellectual property, data and privacy. Finding a workable path through these issues is essential for our security, democracy and economic growth.

As other economists have pointed out, worldwide the 'number one challenge... is to develop growth models that can provide more ample, well-paid, and secure jobs amid a secular re-alignment of the global economy.' And as Nesta's recent *Manifesto for the Creative Economy* argued, the creative industries have the potential to contribute much here. This potential is most likely to be realised if we properly understand the activity and growth patterns of this sector.

In *Risky Business* we argued that policy makers are struggling to enable a twenty-first century economy, at least in part because they are using a nineteenth century map. That the creative industries are missing from our most fundamental economic data sets is only one aspect of the mismatch between Government systems which have their roots in the 1930s or earlier and our modern-day economy.

As we finalised the pamphlet in 2011, some suggested that data was a topic too esoteric to be brought to the top of the agenda. We argued that in the absence of good quality data on the sector, perceptions of unspecified 'riskiness' among financers were making it harder for creative businesses to win the financing they need to grow.

We were delighted with how well the pamphlet was received. And since we published, complementary research and policy activity have shown that improving the quality and quantity of data on the creative industries is indeed an essential and urgent real-world issue. Much has been achieved, but if the UK is to enable promising creative businesses to attract finance and realise their growth potential, the Government and the sector itself must continue to work together to ensure that the 'map' matches the territory.

20 Listening in

Rebuilding the relationship between people and policy

Jamie Bartlett

For Demos, our way of doing research has always been a reflection of our critique of society. People feel disconnected from politics, and believe there is little relationship between their daily experiences and the way decisions are made in Whitehall and Westminster. That means our research has always aimed to involve people meaningfully in projects that might affect them; and to search out new ways to understand people in their natural, lived environments – at home, at work, while shopping, or wherever we find them.

Society and public spaces where people congregate has changed an awful lot since 1993 and consequently so has the way we listen in. When I first joined Demos, in 2008, I recall a colleague expounding the virtues of a new social media platform called 'Twitter'. I guffawed: 'no-one's gonna waste their time on that, mate – trust me'. I now run the first think-tank centre (within Demos) that collates and analyses millions of tweets in real time using complex machine learning algorithms.

Of course, some things haven't changed. Polls – especially national, representative survey data, remain a tried and trusted set of techniques that remain peerless when it comes to statistical rigour. The spirit of the early Demos years (perhaps mindful of its youthful optimism) was to make sure any radical thinking was grounded in weighty data.

In one of our first big interventions, *Freedom's Children* (1995), Geoff Mulgan and Helen Wilkinson used new data from the British Household Panel Survey and MORI/Socioconsult to explore in detail the attitudes of 18 – 34 year olds in Britain. And in November of last year, we launched a major study of multi-dimensional aspects of poverty, using the British Household Panel Survey's modern successor.

Demos was always quick to spot new ways to supplement polling. As Karl Rove was gearing up micro-targeted polling techniques for George W Bush, Demos researchers were busy in Basildon, interviewing 500 skilled workers for *Basildon: the mood of the nation* (2001). Voters there had voted with the country in every election since the 1950s, most famously in 1992.

A poll might give you a decent bird's eye view and some numbers to play with, but there is nothing quite like sitting down for an hour with someone. By homing in on the experiences and aspirations of this crucial swing town, Dennis Hayes and Alan Hudson peered into the country at large, and set out a number of significant trends, which are still playing out today. I am still hopeful we will return to Basildon in 2015.

Getting that richer understanding of people's daily experience would often require going right to where it is, through ethnographic observation. In their 2002 report *Inconvenience Food,* Caroline Hitchman and colleagues conducted interviews with low-income shoppers as they were out doing their weekly shop, who also kept a diary of their eating habits. Listening to people discuss their unease while browsing the frozen food sections led the authors to argue, among other things, that the government needed to do something about making the food chain clearer, more transparent and safer – and given the recent horsemeat scandal, it's hard to disagree.

Occasionally, this approach takes us into unusual places for a think-tank. In *Glasgow 2020*, (2007) Charlie Tims and colleagues asked Glaswegians to describe their aspirations for the city through telling stories. Charlie concluded that hairdressers were a good gauge of local public mood. So much so, in fact, that they were 'the most authentic voice on the high street'. Journalists rather enjoyed that: but Charlie may have been right, and finding new ways of listening to people, especially in their own places of work and life, is a vital part of the research process.

Of course, sometimes we cannot go to where the conversations are – because they are not always happening. Jack Stilgoe and James Wilsdon ran a number of projects looking at how technical and complicated decisions about science policy should involve the public more. In *Nanodialogues* (2007), Jack ran 'people's panels', where 13 uninitiated members of the public took expert witness on nanotechnology and discussed what it meant. And as is usually the case, given a chance, the public will get involved in a thoughtful and insightful way on the most complicated questions of all, and nearly always have something important to add.

Of course, not all research is about understanding society: sometimes it pays to look at the policy makers, and understand their social world, replete with its own pressures, rituals, procedures and absurdities. In 2002 Jake Chapman introduced the world to 'systems thinking' – a way of looking at public services as complex systems full of unintended consequences, and double feedback loops. Jake used a set of new techniques to force policy makers to think about the messy problems they face, expose orthodoxies and work out new solutions.

By 2008, it was impossible to ignore the changing ways in which people – especially young people – were communicating. The falling price of digital technology and the proliferation of broadband access had made available a vast range of ways for young people to express themselves and communicate with each other in video. Much of this was going on under the radar of policy makers and politicians, but it was a dramatic, exciting new space of creativity and expression: video mash-ups, citizen journalism, vlogging, viral video marketing, and community film-making projects. Peter Bradwell and Celia Hannon attended video-making workshops all across Europe and documented this space in *Video Republic*. The power of video may seem obvious now; it was not back then.

That was the year I joined Demos, and by then social media, that conversational, distributed mode of content generation, dissemination and communication, was colonising the social world. You might think that would be a natural place for researchers to look. But its use by think-tanks for research was, and still is, strangely limited. Its potential is enormous.

In 2009, when the English Defence League first burst onto the scene, most commentators saw a modern incarnation of the street-based skinhead groups of the 1970s. But it was in fact rather different: probably more accurately described as a Facebook group with a militant wing. Behind the 500 or so that hit the streets exists a much larger, highly motivated online community of thousands of sympathisers and supporters who set the mood music, recruit, proselytise and organise.

The heartbeat of the movement was its Facebook group, with thousands of fans gossiping, arguing, trolling, organising. This quasi-public space also provided an opportunity to research the group: and by using a new method of direct Facebook surveying, I was able to convince over 1,000 EDL Facebook fans to fill in an online survey, written up in the first ever study of the movement, *Inside the EDL* (2010). The following year I had almost 20,000 survey responses from Facebook supporters of populist left and right-wing parties across Europe, which spawned a series of papers about Beppe Grillo, the Swedish Democrats and the Pirate Party.[1] A decade ago, collecting data of this volume and speed so easily would have been unthinkable.

But even this appears time consuming and laborious compared to more recent changes. Every second, 6,000 tweets are published by people around the world. With easy access to Twitter's Application Programming Interface (API), this remarkable data set is eminently collectable, malleable, understandable. In fact, since 2008 'Twitterology' has grown from a handful to hundreds of research papers, covering everything from topic identification to event detection and political forecasting.[2]

At Demos' the Centre for the Analysis of Social Media – a collaboration with machine learning experts at the University of Sussex – we use artificial intelligence to shape algorithms that can deal with tens of millions of tweets pretty much automatically. In a recent project to understand people's attitudes towards the EU, we built layers of different algorithms working together – some working to get a good sample, some checking whether the tweet was relevant, and others what the tweet meant: three languages, 63 algorithms, and millions of piece of singular insights of people's attitudes. Of course, making sense of these vast, complex and confusing data sets is far more complicated than it appears – but by joining social and computational sciences we are beginning to make sense of this new world in a way that will be of huge benefit to policy makers in the future.

In a sense, then, we are back where we started. Listening to and understanding people's daily experience, in their natural settings and environments – and then translating that into policy making sense – is what Demos has always been about. Demos' founding vision of reconnecting people to politics remains a pressing one. As a research institute, that means going to where people live their lives, whether at work, at home, in the supermarket, at the hairdresser's, or on social networks.

Notes

1 See for example: Bartlett, J, Birdwell, J and Littler, M, *The New Face of Digital Populism*, Demos: London, 2011.

2 Early and emerging examples of twitterology were presented at the International Conference on Web Search and Data Mining 2008.

21 Demos timeline

1993 - 2013

1993

Czechoslovakia splits.

Francis Fukuyama announces *The End of History*.

Murder of Stephen Lawrence.

Maastricht Treaty ratified.

1994

Kurt Cobain found dead.

Channel Tunnel opens.

Nelson Mandela becomes president of South Africa.

First National Lottery numbers drawn.

It is difficult to remember a time when people had so little faith in the political process Demos founding document

Demos launch party, with future PM Tony Blair in attendance

Reconnecting Taxation argues for unitary taxation of multinational companies.

An End to Illusions proposes independence for the Bank of England, written by Alan Duncan MP.

There is a real sense in which Britain has become an 'audit society' Michael Power, **The Audit Explosion**

The Mosaic of Learning by David Hargreaves lays the groundwork for education reform, in what *The Times* calls 'a brilliant pamphlet.'

The World's New Fissures by Vince Cable depicts a world of identity politics beyond left and right; Melanie Phillips finds it 'interesting' in *The Observer*.

1995

Rogue trader topples Barings Bank.

Oklahoma bomb.

OJ Simpson found not guilty.

Blair drops Clause IV.

1996

Deep Blue defeats Gary Kasparov.

Dunblane Massacre.

BSE leads to beef ban.

Dolly the sheep born.

The 'enfant terrible' of think-tanks *The Independent*

Freedom's Children by Helen Wilkinson and Geoff Mulgan describes the downsides of new social freedoms.

The Creative City plots the rise of the creative industries in the UK.

One of those rare pamphlets that help you understand how the world is changing the *FT* on Robert Cooper's **The Post-modern State and the World Order**

Parental Leave recommends the introduction of paid parental leave.

After Social Democracy by John Gray makes the case for a 'communitarian liberalism.'

1997

New Labour election landslide.

Katrina and the Waves win Eurovision.

Hong Kong returns to Chinese control.

Princess Diana dies.

1998

Good Friday agreement.

David Beckham becomes most unpopular man in Britain.

Anthony Giddens finds the Third Way.

Clinton impeached.

Britain's most influential think-tank *The Economist*

Geoff Mulgan goes to No 10 as adviser to the Prime Minister.

Holistic Government Perri 6's call for 'joined-up government' influences Blair's first administration.

Britain™ Mark Leonard reframes the debate on Britain's national identity, described by the *Daily Mail* as 'a blueprint for a national makeover.'

The Proposal suggests that marriages could become 'time-limited.'

Demos offers exactly the sort of long-term thinking that is missing from the current political debate *FT*

The Future of Privacy anticipates public concerns over personal information and privacy.

Animal Rights and Wrongs an essay by Roger Scruton on morality and animals is proclaimed a 'classic' by the *Sunday Telegraph*.

The Good Life recommends that Governments measure people's happiness and quality of life.

1999

First Euro minted.

Minimum wage comes into effect.

NATO involvement in Kosovo conflict begins.

Scottish Parliament and Welsh Assembly created.

2000

Britain survives the millennium bug.

Ken Livingstone becomes first Mayor of London.

Big Brother aired in UK.

George W Bush elected President,
with questions hanging over 'chads.'

One of the education books of the decade *TES* on Tom Bentley's **Learning Beyond the Classroom**

Tom Bentley becomes Director of Demos.

To Our Mutual Advantage outlines the potential of mutuals to transform the economy.

Creating Wealth from Waste sets out a zero waste programme for the UK.

Demos offers the most challenging political agenda for the next century *The Times*

Patient Power by former Conservative Minister Peter Lilley argues that consumer choice could transform the NHS.

Entrepreneurship: the Wired Life describes the rise of portfolio working.

2001

Museums become free to enter.

Foot and mouth closes countryside.

9/11: the Twin Towers are destroyed by a terrorist attack.

David Beckham is redeemed.

2002

Enron and Worldcom go bankrupt.

Golden Jubilee: Bryan May plays the national anthem on top of Buckingham Palace.

Rowan Williams elected Archbishop of Canterbury.

A majority of Britons are now online.

Basildon is a barometer for the mood of the nation

Basildon by Alan Hudson and Dennis Hayes

Politics and Progress, an exploration of citizenship, is written by David Blunkett while serving in Cabinet.

The Protest Ethic by John Lloyd examines the impact of the anti-globalisation movement on the Left.

Governments must learn to think differently

System Failure by Jake Chapman

The Moral Universe Nobel winner Amartya Sen and Mary Midgley call for a remoralisation of politics.

Monarchies, published on the Jubilee, advises that the Queen abdicates.

2003

Space shuttle Columbia crashes.

London introduces the congestion charge.

The Iraq war begins.

Section 28 is repealed.

2004

The Hutton report is published.

The Orange Book attempts to 'reclaim' liberalism.

Fox-hunting banned in England and Wales.

The Boxing Day Tsunami kills over 230,000 people worldwide.

Personalisation is an idea that could be as influential as privatisation was in the 1980s and 1990s in reshaping public provision Charlie Leadbeater

Education Epidemic argues for greater collaboration between schools and is influential in the development of Networked Learning Communities.

The Adaptive State acts as a blueprint for more user-centred public services.

Valuing Culture kicks off a debate on the social value of culture.

Demos makes the first coherent call for 'upstream engagement' — the involvement of non-specialists in setting research priorities Nature

See-through Science is the first in a series of science policy pamphlets, which influence the Government's 10-Year Framework for Science and Innovation.

Personalisation through Participation advocates a radical agenda for personalised public services, featuring a foreword from Schools Minister David Miliband.

Disablism names society's last prejudice.

2005

Jamie Oliver launches his war on turkey twizzlers.

Terrorist attacks on London's transport network.

Bob Geldof and Bono make poverty history at Live 8.

David Cameron elected leader of Conservatives.

2006

Danish cartoons depicting Prophet Mohammed prompt worldwide protests.

Jack Dorsey sends the first ever Tweet.

David Cameron gives his 'hug a hoodie' speech.

Litvinenko dies of polonium poisoning in London.

Everyday democracy means increasing public participation in the formal and informal institutions that shape our daily lives Tom Bentley

True Blue Nicholas Boys Smith makes the case for fair conservatism.

Rebuilding the Public Realm Culture Secretary Tessa Jowell on the need the replenish the 'public.'

National identity may be the best way to preserve the Left's collective ideals David Goodhart, **Progressive Nationalism**

Catherine Fieschi becomes Director of Demos.

Demos' new website wins plaudits, including an award from *Prospect*.

The Other Glass Ceiling uncovers the hidden value of unpaid care work in family life.

Better Humans? explores the implications of human enhancement technologies.

2007

Tony Blair steps down, Gordon Brown becomes PM.

First iPhone goes on sale.

Smoking banned in public places.

Al Gore's *An Inconvenient Truth* wins him a Nobel peace prize.

2008

Thaler and Sunstein give everyone a Nudge.

Boris Johnson elected as Mayor of London.

Northern Rock goes bust, triggering the global financial crisis.

Barack Obama wins the US election.

We can no longer control what others know about us, but we don't understand the consequences FYI

Cultural Diplomacy suggests that Britain's world-class cultural assets should be at the heart of foreign policy.

The Atlas of Ideas explores the new geography of science.

Demos builds urban beach in Bristol.

Demos ideas say a lot about where our public services need to go
Ed Miliband MP

Richard Reeves becomes Director.

The Everyday Democracy Index creates a tool to assess the democratic health of EU countries.

The Politics of Public Behaviour explores how the personal has become political, including contributions from Andy Burnham, Chris Huhne and Andrew Lansley.

2009

UK economy enters recession for the first time since 1991.

MP's expenses scandal.

Global swine flu pandemic.

The Sun switches support to the Conservatives.

2010

Deepwater Horizon oil spill.

David Cameron becomes PM in Britain's first Coalition since the war.

Wikileaks release diplomatic cables.

Mohamed Bouazizi's self-immolation sets off the Arab Spring.

The debate on what we want our society to look like is much richer for Demos' involvement Nick Clegg MP

Demos launches Progressive Conservatism Project led by 'Red Tory' Phillip Blond.

Demos declared 'One to Watch' by *Prospect*.

Service Nation argues for a more holistic approach to citizen service, influencing formation of NCS.

Reinventing the Firm by Will Davies argues we must renew our idea of what a company is for, following the financial crisis.

This is one of the most important findings in a generation David Cameron on **Building Character**

Richard Reeves joins the Cabinet Office as Director of Strategy for Nick Clegg.

Kitty Ussher becomes Director.

Ex Curricula recommends that headteachers should maintain responsibility for excluded pupils — the DfE set up a scheme to ensure just that in 2011.

The Edge of Violence explores the process of radicalisation and has a significant impact on counter-terrorist strategy.

2011

Prince William marries Kate Middleton.

News of the World closes.

Riots in London and across the UK.

Occupy protests across the world.

World population hits 7 billion.

2012

Chris Huhne is charged and resigns from Cabinet.

Facebook reaches 1bn users.

Danny Boyle's opening ceremony launches London 2012.

Leveson report is published.

Social radicals whose time has come again

The Independent

David Goodhart joins as Director.

Demos wins PAN think-tank of the year.

The Forgotten Half defines the 50 per cent of young people that don't go to university, which influences Ed Miliband's 2012 conference speech.

The Entrepeneurial State makes the case for the state playing an active role in the economy, influencing David Willetts MP's Active State agenda.

The current legal status of assisted dying is inadequate and incoherent

concludes the Commission on Assisted Dying, hosted by Demos

Demos launches the Centre for the Analysis of Social Media (CASM) and Demos Finance.

Poverty in Perspective investigates the lived experience of poverty and is welcomed by David Laws MP during major consultation on poverty measure.

#Intelligence predicts the increasing importance of social media intelligence for security services.

2013

Pope Benedict XVI resigns.

Margaret Thatcher dies.

Drummer Lee Rigby is killed in a terrorist attack in Woolwich.

The NSA's PRISM surveillance programme is leaked.

Twenty years of ideas

Demos turns twenty Michael Ignatieff delivers birthday lecture on 'the pressures of progress.'

Demos – Licence to Publish

The work (as defined below) is provided under the terms of this licence ('licence'). The work is protected by copyright and/or other applicable law. Any use of the work other than as authorized under this licence is prohibited. By exercising any rights to the work provided here, you accept and agree to be bound by the terms of this licence. Demos grants you the rights contained here in consideration of your acceptance of such terms and conditions.

1 Definitions

A **'Collective Work'** means a work, such as a periodical issue, anthology or encyclopedia, in which the Work in its entirety in unmodified form, along with a number of other contributions, constituting separate and independent works in themselves, are assembled into a collective whole. A work that constitutes a Collective Work will not be considered a Derivative Work (as defined below) for the purposes of this Licence.

B **'Derivative Work'** means a work based upon the Work or upon the Work and other pre-existing works, such as a musical arrangement, dramatization, fictionalization, motion picture version, sound recording, art reproduction, abridgment, condensation, or any other form in which the Work may be recast, transformed, or adapted, except that a work that constitutes a Collective Work or a translation from English into another language will not be considered a Derivative Work for the purpose of this Licence.

C **'Licensor'** means the individual or entity that offers the Work under the terms of this Licence.

D **'Original Author'** means the individual or entity who created the Work.

E **'Work'** means the copyrightable work of authorship offered under the terms of this Licence.

F **'You'** means an individual or entity exercising rights under this Licence who has not previously violated the terms of this Licence with respect to the Work,or who has received express permission from Demos to exercise rights under this Licence despite a previous violation.

2 Fair Use Rights

Nothing in this licence is intended to reduce, limit, or restrict any rights arising from fair use, first sale or other limitations on the exclusive rights of the copyright owner under copyright law or other applicable laws.

3 Licence Grant

Subject to the terms and conditions of this Licence, Licensor hereby grants You a worldwide, royalty-free, non-exclusive,perpetual (for the duration of the applicable copyright) licence to exercise the rights in the Work as stated below:

A to reproduce the Work, to incorporate the Work into one or more Collective Works, and to reproduce the Work as incorporated in the Collective Works;

B to distribute copies or phonorecords of, display publicly,perform publicly, and perform publicly by means of a digital audio transmission the Work including as incorporated in Collective Works; The above rights may be exercised in all media and formats whether now known or hereafter devised.The above rights include the right to make such modifications as are technically necessary to exercise the rights in other media and formats. All rights not expressly granted by Licensor are hereby reserved.

4 Restrictions

The licence granted in Section 3 above is expressly made subject to and limited by the following restrictions:

A You may distribute,publicly display, publicly perform, or publicly digitally perform the Work only under the terms of this Licence, and You must include a copy of, or the Uniform Resource Identifier for, this Licence with every copy or phonorecord of the Work You distribute, publicly display,publicly perform, or publicly digitally perform.You may not offer or impose any terms on the Work that alter or restrict the terms of this Licence or the recipients' exercise of the rights granted hereunder.You may not sublicence the Work.You must keep intact all notices that refer to this Licence and to the disclaimer of warranties. You may not distribute, publicly display, publicly perform, or publicly digitally perform the Work with any technological measures that control access or use of the Work in a manner inconsistent with the terms of this Licence Agreement.The above applies to the Work as incorporated in a Collective Work, but this does not require the Collective Work apart from the Work itself to be made subject to the terms of this Licence. If You create a Collective Work, upon notice from any Licencor You must, to the extent practicable, remove from the Collective Work any reference to such Licensor or the Original Author, as requested.

B You may not exercise any of the rights granted to You in Section 3 above in any manner that is primarily intended for or directed toward commercial advantage or private monetary compensation.The exchange of the Work for other copyrighted works by means of digital filesharing or otherwise shall not be considered to be intended for or directed toward commercial advantage or private monetary compensation, provided there is no payment of any monetary compensation in connection with the exchange of copyrighted works.

C If you distribute, publicly display, publicly perform, or publicly digitally perform the Work or any Collective Works,You must keep intact all copyright notices for the Work and give the Original Author credit reasonable to the medium or means You are utilizing by conveying the name (or pseudonym if applicable) of the Original Author if supplied; the title of the Work if supplied. Such credit may be implemented in any reasonable manner; provided, however, that in the case of a Collective Work, at a minimum such credit will appear where any other comparable authorship credit appears and in a manner at least as prominent as such other comparable authorship credit.

5 Representations, Warranties and Disclaimer

A By offering the Work for public release under this Licence, Licensor represents and warrants that, to the best of Licensor's knowledge after reasonable inquiry:

i Licensor has secured all rights in the Work necessary to grant the licence rights hereunder and to permit the lawful exercise of the rights granted hereunder without You having any obligation to pay any royalties, compulsory licence fees, residuals or any other payments;

ii The Work does not infringe the copyright, trademark, publicity rights, common law rights or any other right of any third party or constitute defamation, invasion of privacy or other tortious injury to any third party.

B except as expressly stated in this licence or otherwise agreed in writing or required by applicable law,the work is licenced on an 'as is'basis,without warranties of any kind, either express or implied including,without limitation,any warranties regarding the contents or accuracy of the work.

6 Limitation on Liability

Except to the extent required by applicable law, and except for damages arising from liability to a third party resulting from breach of the warranties in section 5, in no event will licensor be liable to you on any legal theory for any special, incidental,consequential, punitive or exemplary damages arising out of this licence or the use of the work, even if licensor has been advised of the possibility of such damages.

7 Termination

A This Licence and the rights granted hereunder will terminate automatically upon any breach by You of the terms of this Licence. Individuals or entities who have received Collective Works from You under this Licence,however, will not have their licences terminated provided such individuals or entities remain in full compliance with those licences. Sections 1, 2, 5, 6, 7, and 8 will survive any termination of this Licence.

B Subject to the above terms and conditions, the licence granted here is perpetual (for the duration of the applicable copyright in the Work). Notwithstanding the above, Licensor reserves the right to release the Work under different licence terms or to stop distributing the Work at any time; provided, however that any such election will not serve to withdraw this Licence (or any other licence that has been, or is required to be, granted under the terms of this Licence), and this Licence will continue in full force and effect unless terminated as stated above.

8 Miscellaneous

A Each time You distribute or publicly digitally perform the Work or a Collective Work, Demos offers to the recipient a licence to the Work on the same terms and conditions as the licence granted to You under this Licence.

B If any provision of this Licence is invalid or unenforceable under applicable law, it shall not affect the validity or enforceability of the remainder of the terms of this Licence, and without further action by the parties to this agreement, such provision shall be reformed to the minimum extent necessary to make such provision valid and enforceable.

C No term or provision of this Licence shall be deemed waived and no breach consented to unless such waiver or consent shall be in writing and signed by the party to be charged with such waiver or consent.

D This Licence constitutes the entire agreement between the parties with respect to the Work licensed here.There are no understandings, agreements or representations with respect to the Work not specified here. Licensor shall not be bound by any additional provisions that may appear in any communication from You.This Licence may not be modified without the mutual written agreement of Demos and You.